HEALTHY STABLES
BY DESIGN

HEALTHY STABLES
BY DESIGN

A Common Sense Approach
to the Health and Safety of Horses

For Eugenia,

Thanks for introducing to Hechole,
to the world of horses,

John Blackburn 2017

By John Blackburn   images Publishing   with Beth Herman

Published in Australia in 2013 by

The Images Publishing Group Pty Ltd

ABN 89 059 734 431

6 Bastow Place, Mulgrave, Victoria 3170, Australia

Tel: +61 3 9561 5544 Fax: +61 3 9561 4860

books@imagespublishing.com

www.imagespublishing.com

Copyright © The Images Publishing Group Pty Ltd 2013

The Images Publishing Group Reference Number: 1076

National Library of Australia Cataloguing-in-Publication entry

Author:	Blackburn, John, author.
Title:	Healthy stables by design : a common sense approach to the health and safety of horses / John Blackburn with Beth Herman.
ISBN:	978 1 86470 515 7 (hardback)
Subjects:	Horses – Housing – Safety measures.
	Horses – Housing – Health aspects.
	Horses – Housing – Design.
	Stables – Safety measures.
	Stables – Health aspects.
	Stables – Design.
Other Authors/Contributors:	Herman, Beth author.
Dewey Number:	636.10831

Edited by Mandy Herbet

Designed by The Graphic Image Studio Pty Ltd, Mulgrave, Australia

www.tgis.com.au

Pre-publishing services by United Graphic Pte Ltd, Singapore

Printed on 150gsm G-print smooth by Everbest Printing Co. Ltd., in Hong Kong/China

CONTENTS

GENDER DISCLAIMER

The reader will discover that horses are generally referred to as "him" in this book for uniformity. In no way is this to be interpreted as sexism—a sleight of mares or fillies. It becomes awkward and cumbersome to repeatedly say "him or her," or "his or hers," and I have gone to great lengths never to refer to these sentient beings as "it." Animal advocates the world over caution against using "it" in their continuing quest to educate human beings about issues of neglect and abuse—that these creatures are not unfeeling objects like clothing or furniture ("it") so easily cast aside.

FOREWORD

As Founder and CEO of a global sports performance business I started right out of college, it's fair to say I'm accustomed to meeting extreme challenges every day. With more than 5,000 employees worldwide to date, our business model is predicated on building a great product, telling a great story, servicing the business, and cultivating a great team. With all of that, I've said for years I was always smart enough to be naïve enough to not know what we could not accomplish. We work hard, dream big, are passionate about what we do, and believe consistently in the possibilities.

In 2007, inspired to execute some long held dreams of a foray into Thoroughbred breeding and racing, and with a practiced blind eye to what we could not accomplish, I purchased Glyndon, Maryland's Sagamore Farm. It's the former home to Alfred G. Vanderbilt and a legion of explosive race horses including Native Dancer, Discovery, and Bed O'Roses. These celebrated equines were buried on-site and provided quite a legacy.

It was clear that to become as much of a contender in racing as we are in business, we'd need to build a winning environment. At 530 acres and with multiple massive structures on the property, many of which pre-dated The Great Depression and even World War I, this property required a painstaking renovation of each horse barn, bringing them up to modern standards, while also preserving their historical provenance. Though I was adept at running a global sports performance business, the strategic Sagamore Farm redesign with an eye to the future and homage to the past would be no easy feat.

To that end, my meeting with equestrian architect John Blackburn proved highly beneficial. I was impressed by his passion and reputation for designing horse farms that promote the health and safety of horses, but also meet a level of design standards that convey an appreciation for quality and a reverence for the land. Although I had my own agenda, I learned a great deal about

the confluence of architecture and scientific principles—such as aerodynamic ventilation and strategic natural light—that would create optimal conditions for our broodmares, foals, yearlings, two-year-olds and up, and for our hard-working employees as well. With a goal to someday win the Triple Crown, it was imperative to establish an environment that facilitated a competitive edge— and we found that in John's designs. What's more, he was able to execute this vision while preserving the historical fabric of each barn, something important to me as a Maryland native and as a steward of Sagamore Farm's legacy.

To paraphrase a favorite Sun Tzu *The Art of War* tenet of mine, which refers to the victorious Army attacking the defeated enemy, the game is already won or lost by the way you approach it.

Our vision is to be number one both in business and horse racing. We are confident in our approach—and grateful to John Blackburn for helping us get there.

Kevin Plank, Founder and CEO
Under Armour

PREFACE

A dog may be man's best friend, but the horse wrote history.
Author unknown

For thousands of years the horse has worked for us. In conditions ranging from fierce battles to fierce weather and everything in between, the horse has built railroads and cities (ancient and otherwise), towed bricks and boulders, pulled plows, and ferried ammunition, carrying the U.S. mail at breakneck speed. By their nature they've opened hearts and territories. Their contribution is unparalleled, and they were often the thin line between life and death for their owners. In the Old West, horses were so valuable that horse theft was considered a hanging offense. And in some cultures, it is said we owe these vigorous creatures a debt that can never be repaid. In any culture they deserve to be cared for and protected.

Following early domestication horses became an investment of the purse, so to speak, and, for the lucky individuals who understood the connection between horse and rider, one of the heart as well. Though considered chattel with negligible rights and recourse by virtue of many of the laws written to "protect" them—some on the books for as many as 300 years—more fortunate animals have owners who've recognized their gifts and natural abilities, with nurturing and protection of these paramount.

The universe is full of good ideas and this book is not intended as a treatise on absolute design of horse barns. However, in 30 years it's fair to say I've learned something about the difference between good stabling and bad the latter of which I firmly believe can border on criminal treatment of equines. Among the many requisites for an exceptional barn design, issues of strategic ventilation and natural light affect the health and safety of horses and are high on the agenda. No one would think twice about building a house that provided comfort and protection for its human inhabitants, so why should shelter for horses be any different? At the same time, it is important to differentiate that creating an environment for a human is not the same as creating one for a horse. A human environment would be unhealthy and counterproductive for the latter. Our primary concern should be the animal's health and appropriate conditions, which can be compounded when two or more are stabled together, with the best environment one that closely approximates nature.

In reading this book, it may be important to make a connection between what was done in the past for the stabling of horses and what I do as an equestrian architect.

Something about History

It's important to note that, by nature, a horse was meant to live in the wild. Philosopher Herbert Spencer's aptly-coined "survival of the fittest" evolutionary theory describes an environmentally-driven process over millions of years that adapts an animal to its surroundings, and the horse is no exception. When we began to domesticate the horse and bring him into captivity and "shelter," though again our intent may have been to nurture and protect our financial and emotional investment (maybe even more so in modern times), in actuality we risk(ed) doing the horse, and consequently ourselves, more harm than good. As it turns out, conventional ideas of stabling more often than not challenge and contradict natural equine instincts.

Realistically, it may have taken centuries for an understanding of what protection actually meant other than simple feeding and containment. While a degree of predictability as a result of domestication is present in these animals, a certain wildness will always be there because of the horse's instinct to protect himself—his only means of serious defense being flight.

Horses' behavior can be erratic but in my opinion that's what makes them even more beautiful, dynamic creatures. That is also what makes stable design critical to protect this kind of investment. The stable should be designed to put the horse at ease in what is traditionally an unnatural and unhealthy environment. I've always said if you give a horse half a chance to injure himself he'll find a way to do it. When you bring him into captivity, this condition is exacerbated as you limit his freedom to choose and/or find a way out. A horse's instinct is to flee perceived danger to a safe environment, and conventional stabling, though a necessity, may not be the safest environment.

For example a simple preventive measure like a yoke gate—used in many of our barn designs—affords a startled horse who may try to flee (and injure himself) the opportunity to look out from a stall, up and down an aisle, in response to a noise or other disruption, for assurance that all is well. It also allows him to socialize with others of his kind, which, as herd animals, provides a measure of comfort.

In ancient Greece and Rome much of our data points to accounts of necessary military stabling, with extant texts recognizing the unnaturalness of stabling in the first place under other conditions. When owners did build, sources such as Roman scholar Marcus Terentius Varro wrote in his Rerum Rusticarum Libri Tres—a discourse on farming practices and principles—of the importance of stabling far away from swamps and marshlands. In this environment, he said, "... minute creatures (a precursor to microbiology and epidemiology) which cannot be seen by the eyes...can float through the air and enter the body through the mouth and nose and cause serious diseases." (Varro Rerum Rusticarum On Agriculture 1.12.2) In building modern stables that address the health and safety of horses, as will be evident in the ensuing chapters we go to great lengths to site our barns so that environmental factors work with and for rather than against the horse, something not always considered in the average horse barn.

Finally, while horses still play traditional roles on farms and ranches, in modern society that role has expanded to include widespread participation in sports, entertainment, as general companion animals, in the medical realm as therapeutic riding partners, and more. As humans continue to rely on horses we must continue our search for safer and healthier ways to care for them.

As you read this book, I hope you will come to appreciate the level of care and planning intrinsic to stable design for the life of the horse and the safety of the equestrian—and how both must work together for optimal results. Promoting the health and safety of horses through design has become my life's work, and the results can work for you.

INTRODUCTION

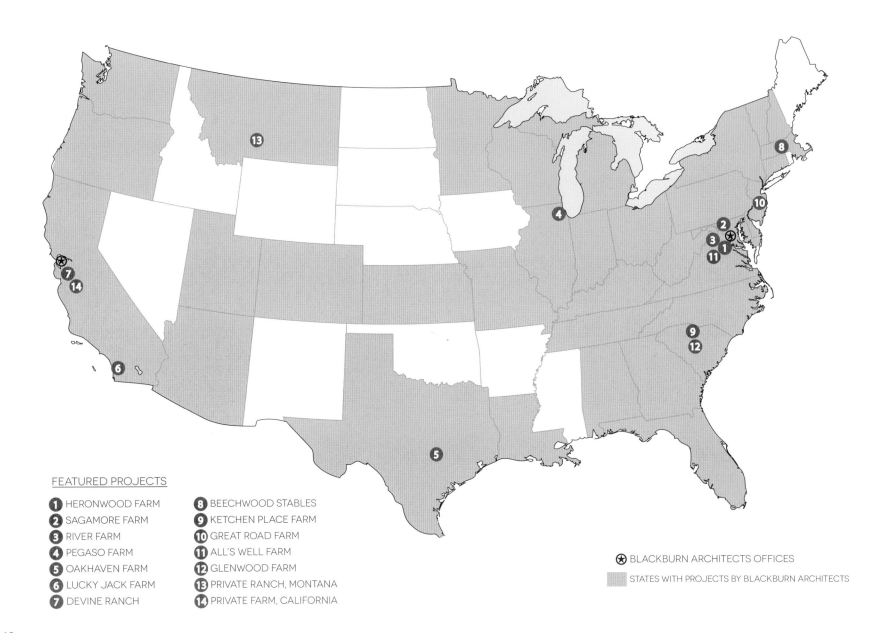

FEATURED PROJECTS

1 HERONWOOD FARM
2 SAGAMORE FARM
3 RIVER FARM
4 PEGASO FARM
5 OAKHAVEN FARM
6 LUCKY JACK FARM
7 DEVINE RANCH

8 BEECHWOOD STABLES
9 KETCHEN PLACE FARM
10 GREAT ROAD FARM
11 ALL'S WELL FARM
12 GLENWOOD FARM
13 PRIVATE RANCH, MONTANA
14 PRIVATE FARM, CALIFORNIA

⊛ BLACKBURN ARCHITECTS OFFICES

☐ STATES WITH PROJECTS BY BLACKBURN ARCHITECTS

While designing for the health and safety of horses is clearly my life's work, it certainly didn't start out that way.

As a child growing up in small town East Tennessee, horses were part of our lives though frankly I had no interest in riding them properly or understanding more than the fundamental fact that they needed food to survive. Except for the occasional bareback sprint across an open field, our neighbor's utilitarian barn loft held sufficient allure for me through the sweltering days of a typical Appalachian summer. I willingly left all manner of formal riding and equine analysis to my twin sister, who doted on a Tennessee Walking Horse named Dixie.

In the late 1960s, I traded a semi-rural life to study architecture at Clemson University, located in an even smaller town than the one I was from. I followed up with a master's degree in urban design from St. Louis' Washington University, desiring a more sophisticated life away from the limited environment in which I was raised. An interest in designing buildings inspired by their context, environment, and function began at Clemson University where I was exposed to architect Louis Sullivan's "form (ever) follows function," and Mies van der Rohe's "less is more."

Accordingly, I immersed myself in the civilized world of urban design, using my surroundings as the catalyst for structures driven by the way they would be used, viewed, and placed in the cityscape. Convinced I was light years away from the barn and anything equine in this respect, a strategized move to ply my craft in Washington, D.C. underscored my intentions for a life devoid of hay and halters. Little did I know destiny had something else in store.

As a young architect in the mid-1980s, and while moonlighting from my day job, former colleague Robbie Smith and I decided to officially join forces when a tip came about a substantial horse project on 400 acres near Middleburg, Virginia. Discovering that renowned landscape architect Morgan Wheelock was to plan the farm and would require an architect to design its structures, it mattered little to him that we'd never designed a horse farm. At that point we had nothing to show Wheelock, who was intimately familiar with horse farms and their impact on the welfare of the horse, or the prospective client—a successful D.C. real estate developer—except a meager portfolio of porch additions, a hot dog kiosk, and garages. Nevertheless this was an opportunity to work and we had nothing to lose by auditioning, so to speak.

A Middleburg native who was acquainted with the region's building style, my then-partner Robbie Smith resourcefully photographed the forms and materials used in area residences and commercial structures, as well as barns. Many were easily 100 years old and probably not designed by an architect, though strongly represented the region in their style, scale, context, and functionality— echoes of Louis Sullivan's "form (ever) follows function." We took the photographs and projected slides of them onto the wall of our tiny third floor unfurnished walk-up office, traced over them, and transferred the images to (pre-PowerPoint) illustration boards in a series of hand-drawn sketches. These would serve as our "portfolio" presentation. Somehow we won the commission, suddenly finding ourselves with eight buildings to design and, as a result of our shotgun wedding to equestrian architecture, firmly on a course that would change both our lives and the lives of many hundreds of horses and their owners.

To be sure, barns are often perceived as dark, dusty, uninviting structures. However it's also widely understood among equestrians that the best environment for a horse—beyond the great outdoors where their instincts are freely cultivated and exercised—is an environment that reflects the same. Wheelock's formulas bridged inconsistencies, in many cases defying common barn convention, with a design theory focused on creating natural light and ventilation within the barn. These changes helped preclude incidents of fatal barn fires and other accidents, created ideal environments to manage equine allergies, overall respiratory health and reproduction issues, and impacted horses' instincts and behaviors as they related to sheltering. In short, Wheelock's hypotheses were simple, yet revolutionary.

All said, we were two young architects with an interest in designing to fit a context and were inspired by Wheelock's theories to let the natural environment (and not just the built one) be that context, long before it became fashionable to do so. Wheelock and the owner probably saw a couple of young professionals with open minds and a willingness to learn, needing to jumpstart their careers by putting into practice the former's ideas.

More than a quarter century later, with the design of more than 160 horse farms and facilities in our portfolio including Maryland's historical Sagamore Farm (former home of Alfred G. Vanderbilt's Native Dancer), my firm is at the forefront of an architectural niche that can and has empowered many of the nation's two million horse owners. Credited with raising the bar on barn design through strategic use of elements such as aerodynamic principles and passive solar heating and cooling, our goal is to ensure the health and safety of horses through design. We like to say that in every project there are three things: the site; the owner; the horse. While the first two may change, care and concern for the animal never does. That's the common thread that goes through all of our work. We've been riding that horse for 30 years.

John Blackburn, AIA, Washington, D.C.

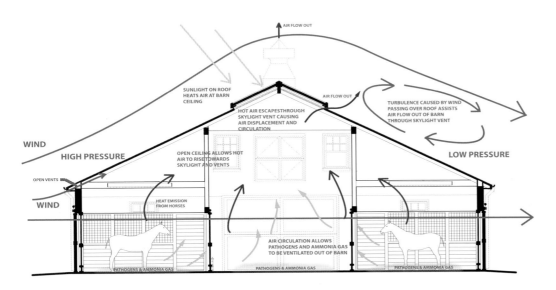

WIND

HIGH PRESSURE

OPEN VENTS

WIND

AIR FLOW OUT

SUNLIGHT ON ROOF HEATS AIR AT BARN CEILING

AIR FLOW OUT

HOT AIR ESCAPES THROUGH SKYLIGHT VENT CAUSING AIR DISPLACEMENT AND CIRCULATION

TURBULENCE CAUSED BY WIND PASSING OVER ROOF ASSISTS AIR FLOW OUT OF BARN THROUGH SKYLIGHT VENT

LOW PRESSURE

OPEN CEILING ALLOWS HOT AIR TO RISE TOWARDS SKYLIGHT AND VENTS

HEAT EMISSION FROM HORSES

AIR CIRCULATION ALLOWS PATHOGENS AND AMMONIA GAS TO BE VENTILATED OUT OF BARN

PATHOGENS & AMMONIA GAS

PATHOGENS & AMMONIA GAS

PATHOGENS & AMMONIA GAS

SELECTED PROJECTS

HERONWOOD FARM
square one

Natural light and natural ventilation

are the two most critical concerns

when designing for horses.

John Blackburn

Heronwood Farm is where it all began. Located in Upperville, Virginia, part of the bucolic Middleburg region, the farm's 400-plus acres were previously owned by entrepreneur and Redskins owner Jack Kent Cooke, and my former partner, Robbie Smith, and I were retained in 1983 by its subsequent owner to create eight initial buildings. These included two major barns: broodmare and yearling; three small isolation barns; a service building with bunk house; a large storage building for hay and bedding; and a manager's house.

Taking our cue and those first tenuous steps into the world of specialized barn design from Morgan Wheelock, the Cambridge,

Massachusetts-based landscape architect who'd been commissioned to design the site, we incorporated his theories of natural light and ventilation into the 20-stall, 9,400-square-foot broodmare barn and 16-stall, 7,900-square-foot yearling barn. Wheelock's practices, which had improved the health and safety of horses in the U.S., Canada, and France, helped broodmares to cycle naturally and carry their foals to full term without the fire danger and added cost of continuous, overburdened artificial lighting, sometimes used as a stimulant. His passive barn systems also helped ensure that equines avoided acquiring and transmitting respiratory ailments to the entire barn, as they are known to do. Typically this is attributed to a direct result of conventional barn ventilation, which is horizontal and achieved by opening the front and back doors to catch the breeze. In this manner, each horse catches whatever may be airborne from the previous horse. Random, ubiquitous, and ill-placed fans, which are a common feature of many barns, only serve to exacerbate the process by circulating bacteria, pathogens, allergens, and disease. To alter these standards, Wheelock advocated siting barns perpendicular to the prevailing summer breeze, something that precluded sick barns.

At Heronwood we utilized low vents and vented skylights—in fact, this project marked our first use of a vented skylight in a barn— as well as heated (by the sun) roofs and eaves to encourage upward ventilation. These principles were largely based on 18th-century Dutch-Swiss mathematician **Daniel Bernoulli's equation of vertical lift**—created by the speed

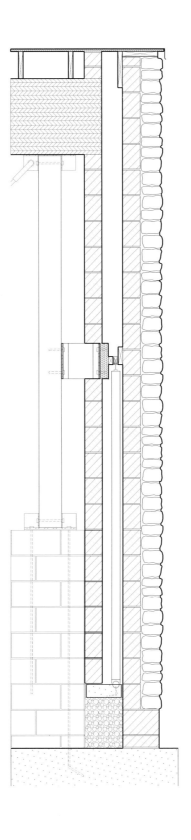

of airflow over an airplane wing. The result we were looking for in our design was also facilitated by the rise of hot air known as the **chimney effect**, where air is pulled in low and vented out high. By constitution horses give off a lot of body heat and humidity. Along with the heat of the sun on the roof and skylight, this creates a heat differential between the barn floor and roof ridge. As heat rises, the Bernoulli effect helps move it along as the prevailing breeze blows across the roof.

Arriving at Heronwood in those early days, we were struck by the prevalence of stone walls or fences that stretched as far as the eye could see—accidental monuments, in a manner of speaking, to the enterprising farmers and their descendants who had cultivated and maintained the land and livestock for generations. In colonial days, occupants would take the rocks from their fields and pile them up to create fence lines. Because the existing fence lines would not work with the new paddock arrangement, however, Wheelock dismantled the fences and we paid homage to the past by preserving the stones for use in the new buildings.

Desiring to emulate the characteristic Federal-style architecture that defined the Middleburg countryside, we used that form as gabled end structures, dormers, and other features in our buildings. The big question at the time was how to take the shape and proportion that came from a residential design element and

0   40ft

apply it to horse shelters, which may be 200 to 250 feet long, 35 to 40 feet high, and 35-plus feet wide. In other words, how do we take the Federal-style scale and context, apply it to a barn, and actually have it work both aesthetically and in a practical sense?

We achieved this, in part, by using the dismantled stone fences, along with locally sourced stone (from Virginia and West Virginia) to create a shape at the end of the broodmare barn that imitated the Federal form, shape, and proportion. This element became a recess to contain the barn's pocket doors, emerging as a dominant form in the building that became highly functional as well. In addition the same shape was repeated in the dormer windows and other gabled roof forms.

Design-wise, we learned that psychology is integral to the layout of a broodmare barn. It needs to be approached from the center through a meeting place or reception room in which the prospective customer can relax and learn about a horse's stock or bloodlines. In a 20- to 24-stall barn, that reception room is typically located near the center of the barn's long axis to balance the stalls on each end for more efficient service by the grooms.

At Heronwood, well-appointed furnishings provided for the ease and comfort of visitors, as there's no denying that value in the interior translates to value in the quality of the product being sold. Conversely, with the yearling barn, the animal himself is being sold as opposed to strictly the bloodlines, so there is less emphasis on a luxe interior as the horse tends to be observed outdoors. Here, Wheelock designed a well-landscaped and pristine show ring centered on the cross aisle of the yearling barn.

Clearly the most imposing and intriguing aspect of the broodmare barn's interior, and perhaps its exterior, is the ridge skylight that runs nearly the entire length of the roof and barn. In our quest to saturate the building with natural light—something elemental to efficient cycling of the broodmare—we decided a series of skylights might do the job, but what is essentially a glass ceiling or continuous skylight would achieve the objective seamlessly. In a broodmare barn, and in thoroughbred breeding, ideal conditions—those that don't

just simulate but actually invite natural conditions indoors—facilitate the horse cycling and foal dropping as early in the season after January 1st as possible. Because a horse is classified as a yearling on the following January 1st, regardless of when he was born in the previous year, one that has been on the ground and living/training longer when designated as such tends to be a stronger horse. In this regard, a barn created to court nature provides optimal opportunities for efficient and expedient fertility earlier in the year.

Additionally, without skylights and their benefits, handlers are known to enter dark barns, turning on lights at 4 a.m., to simulate a sunrise. Lights may go unrecognized and remain on all day, building up heat, igniting nests and cobwebs, inflating operating costs, and surely increasing the risk of a major barn fire.

As thoroughbreds are delicate animals with sensitive respiratory systems, keeping them extremely healthy and less susceptible to infection was paramount to the barn's ventilation. Accordingly, it was sited perpendicular to the prevailing summer breeze so as not to encourage airborne bacteria pathogens, and allergens to travel through. Next, employing the aforementioned chimney effect and fluid dynamics principles of Daniel Bernoulli, vertical lift, or an upward airflow, was attained by placing vents along the floor and utilizing vented skylights, heated by the sun (which also heats the roof and eaves), which cause the heat within the barn to rise and exit. Horses typically suffer more health issues due to heat intolerance than they do in colder weather—except in extreme conditions.

Using a definite 7:12 roof pitch as we did also discouraged heated air from radiating back down, the way it would with many prefabricated barns that employ a 3:12 pitch that in fact makes the barn hotter instead of cooler. With the 7:12 pitch, heat travels up toward the vented skylight, creating the desired airflow and cooling. At Heronwood we learned that on a hot August afternoon, even without the wind outside, you could stand in the main aisle of the barn and feel

your hair lift just from the natural movement of air created by chimney and Bernoulli effects working together.

Storage is a serious consideration when designing barns that address the health and safety of horses. More fatal barn accidents occur because of improper placement of hay, grain, bedding, and other flammable elements, which are generally stored overhead, creating imminent fire hazards. Additionally, hay stored in this manner contributes to widespread allergens and other equine respiratory ailments as the horse consistently inhales particles from above. In this respect, and considering Heronwood Farm was a fairly large thoroughbred breeding operation with multiple staff, it was better to isolate

and confine the hay and bedding to one centralized area than to break it up into smaller components and facilities. In this manner, load was reduced on farm roads for big feed trucks going in and out, and outsiders were kept to a service area located, in this case, adjacent to the road. Consequently, farm security was less of an issue with its additional operating costs.

At the owner's request, barns were masonry block as he wanted them to be fire safe and durable. While we considered using brick in a nod to more popular regional building materials, and also looked at wood for its aesthetic, masonry block with stucco applied to the exterior created a clean look that satisfied everyone. What's more, stucco is not alien to the area as it was used on many structures in previous eras. Stone was used

for its richness in the base, on the ends in deference to Middleburg/Upperville's Federal-style architecture, and in the cross aisle entrances. Again, it's the psychology of rich materials that tie into the landscape that make for a strong statement.

Because the owner did not want Dutch doors on the exterior side of the stalls, preferring the cleaner look of the long side of the barn, we put in low wall vents with dampers to aid and control airflow. This achieved many of the same results as the Dutch door. We also used Hopper windows, which open inside instead of out, but placed them strategically where the lowest point was about 12 feet up to preclude injury if a horse reared up in the stall. Hopper windows served to route the incoming air up to facilitate ventilation.

In subsequent years, Heronwood Farm saw the construction of an enclosed, covered round pen, a renovation/addition to the owner's office and also to his residence, additional staff housing, adaptive reuse of an old residence on an adjoining farm that the owner purchased for staff housing and a farm office, renovation of a private estate barn for private/recreational horses, and renovations to grandstands and designs for judges' stands at the Upperville Horse Show grounds—site of the oldest horse show in the country and part of Heronwood.

The barns stand as a testament to our first application of design principles that promote the health and safety of horses.

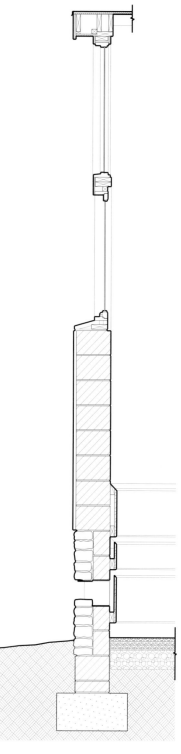

SAGAMORE FARM
a time for titans

There's nothing more thrilling than racing, and the homestretch is where you can see it, hear it, smell it, and feel it.

John Blackburn

Storied and iconic Sagamore Farm, established in 1925 by Bromo-Seltzer inventor Isaac Emerson and a 21st birthday gift to Alfred G. Vanderbilt II from his mother, who was Emerson's daughter, in 1933, had been home to a virtual equine Who's Who. Elite equines including Bed o'Roses, Discovery, and Vanderbilt's revered Native Dancer—a titan among racehorses—put the farm on a stratospheric racing map for decades. Winning 21 out of 22 races and missing the Triple Crown by only a nose, Native Dancer had won his owner's heart in the process. Though notoriously stoic by nature, Vanderbilt was reportedly deeply affected by his beloved horse's death in 1967, burying the fabled "Galloping Gray Ghost" on the property in toto (as opposed to the more traditional head, hoofs, and heart common at other farms), along with his halter, blanket, and bag of treats.

At the time of its sale in 1986 to an area real estate developer, and at about 530 acres, the Glyndon, Maryland property had deteriorated considerably, falling victim to the state racing industry's revised federal tax laws and recession. With an eye to the future, the new owner had intended to subdivide Sagamore Farm into home sites, a proposition vehemently rejected by the historic-minded community. Subsequently leasing several of the old barns to thoroughbred breeding and training entities, in the late 1990s the owner commissioned Blackburn Architects to turn a portion of the farm into a private home and equestrian center for his wife, along with building a party barn naturally for entertainment purposes.

Following completion of the master plan, the owner decided to move and the farm was sold in 2007 to Maryland native son, University of Maryland football hero, and founder/CEO Kevin Plank of Under Armour sports apparel—a business he'd started 11 years earlier with a reported $17,000 from a campus flower delivery service. Today it earns revenues of nearly $2 billion.

With a goal to help revitalize the state's racing industry, Plank's mandate in also retaining Blackburn Architects was to transform the decaying historical landmark— to which he soon added 100 acres when purchasing a baronial mansion and grounds that overlooked his property for meeting and function space—into a

peerless 21st century breeding and training operation, without sacrificing its provenance. In fact, true to form and emblematic of what has made Plank as much of a maverick in his world as Native Dancer was in his, Plank deftly drafted his own multi-phased vision and mission statements—the latter to win the Triple Crown and the former addressing the restoration/redesign of the 530-acre farm's infrastructure, barns, facilities, and grounds. In short, he wanted to return the property to its original glory, but with modern innovations that made paramount the health and safety of his horses, thereby establishing Sagamore Farm, in his words, "as the preeminent horse facility in the State of Maryland and the United States."

With a 15- to 20-year master plan before us, input from Plank's general manager, Tom Mullikin, factored in addressing the health, safety, comfort, and productivity

of Sagamore Farm's thoroughbred population. A horse aficionado and high school classmate of Plank's, Mullikin had jettisoned an IT job with a major company for seemingly greener (equine) pastures in Kentucky, before being lured back home by Plank.

At Sagamore, our first order of business was to redesign an existing 20-stall, 9,130-square foot broodmare barn and 16-stall, 7,455-square-foot foaling barn, with designs that reflected one another. In anticipation of a new road and service entrance still to be built in the future, which will impact transport of these horses, the broodmare and foaling barns were flipped, so to speak, for logistics and functional purposes, where one became the other.

While a prodigious use of natural light and ventilation were high on the agenda, once again paying homage to the historical

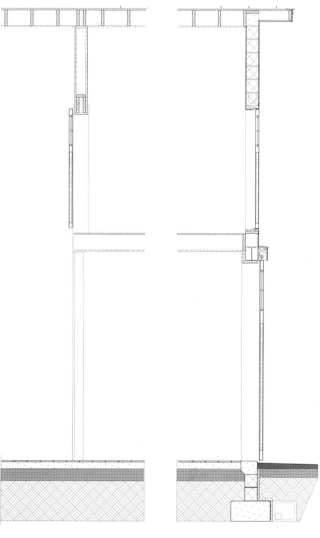

aesthetic of the existing structures—and largely their exteriors which were painted with the farm's red and white racing colors— was tantamount to any modern updates.

When we started, the broodmare and foaling barns were extremely dark and dank—truly miserable spaces though some of the best horses in thoroughbred racing history had been raised there. Basically gutting their interiors, we also reduced the size of excessive 16-by-16-foot stalls to approximately 14-by-15 feet, deciding more stalls of a more reasonable size were beneficial to the long-term goals of the farm.

Continuous overhead haylofts, which are imminent fire and respiratory hazards, were removed, and a vented ridge skylight

the length of each barn was added. Storage areas, created at the very ends of the barns, also reaped the benefits of the massive skylights to decrease the risk of incendiary materials, such as hay and bedding, igniting from the extended use of artificial lighting.

Skylight and roof ventilation, along with lower vents (in this case we used Dutch doors and eave vents) ensure that the horses' own body heat and moisture, along with any barn bacteria, allergens, and pathogens, will rise to the top and exit the structure. Rather than placing fans at the entrances to barns or at the front of the stall as is typical, a practice that expedites the transmission of airborne ailments from one horse to another, the fans here were placed high on walls, directed into only one area of a stall, enabling the horse to move in and out of the breeze as needed.

Where the vented roof and skylight were concerned, Mullikan expressed concern that with too much ventilation—where wind blows in from across the field and across the roof, and mist, rain or particles of snow may enter through the louvers or vents, involving the aisles—horses would be negatively affected. However, in our quest to replicate nature, an environment to which the horse is best adapted, the temperature inside the barn should be within 8 to 10 degrees of the outside temperature—except in extreme conditions—which is the structure's primary purpose. While we do not necessarily court rain and snow in the interior, to an equine these occurrences are as natural as anything else.

Furthering that concept, as horses adapt more readily to cold than heat, because Maryland's summer climate is traditionally hot and humid

the means to cool them down was paramount in Sagamore's barn designs. Unfortunately, as the barns were existing structures, it was not possible to site them perpendicular to the prevailing summer breeze, though they were not too far off from where we would have built them.

Opening up enclosed stalls and adding Dutch doors along the exterior allowed us to vent air in low, in lieu of perfect siting, and both barns easily went from dark to bright. Broodmares were also ensured as much as light as possible early in the season for optimal natural cycling and foaling, as the use of extended periods of artificial lighting for this purpose is not as effective and clearly presents a barn fire hazard and additional operational cost.

Additionally, the inclusion of exterior Dutch doors facilitated swift egress in the event of a fire, where people and frightened equines do not have to worry about navigating long

aisles to flee the structure. Much to his credit, by putting the comfort, health, and safety of his thoroughbreds above all else, Plank forfeited historical tax credits on these barns which may have accrued had we not altered the barns' envelope using Dutch doors, though we did so minimally.

In continued efforts to preserve the barns' authentic fabric, we chose not to alter the existing rooflines for optimal heat rise and ventilation even though they had a 5:12 slope instead of the recommended 7:12 slope. Doors and windows on the ends of the barn had, somewhere in previous years, been changed from their original form, so copious research allowed us to restore them to their historical roots. We also removed old chimney flues as coal and wood burning stoves had long since been retired.

Though we'd indeed gutted the barns' decayed interiors for the renovation, Plank very much wanted to salvage and reuse as many of the

original materials as possible. Accordingly, some of the old wood reemerged in millwork that included tack room cabinets, desks, and storage places, and was repurposed in interior railings. Recycled paver flooring was used, along with recycled steel in stall systems. Preservation of both barns' existing exterior concrete block frames and roof framing, as well as insulated barn offices to reduce energy waste, were part of the new design.

For a time, because some of the other barns on the property are wood frame with board-and-batten siding and we wanted a uniformity of design, we considered siding for the broodmare and foaling barns. We ultimately retained the original stucco however, though incursions into the material resulted from the installation of the Dutch doors. Patching and painting provided good results in the end.

Lastly, a brand new 24-stall, 7,200-square-foot yearling barn in the spirit of the other

two was more recently completed, built on the footprint of what was there previously. Fourteen miles of white fencing frame these magnificent buildings and pastures, and improved gateways and newly created paddocks have also been produced.

Separate from Blackburn Architects' efforts, Plank upgraded an existing ¾-mile training track. While most tracks today are made at least in part from shredded plastic, rubber, and the like, Under Armour hoisted the recycling flag a little higher and created a track comprised of packed fibers from recycled scraps of its sports clothing.

Though much of Sagamore Farm's restoration and redesign is currently on hold, yielding to the owner's focus on training and building breeding stock, the master plan includes restoring a former behemoth—an oval-shaped 90-stall training barn containing a quarter-mile indoor track. The farm operation will likely not require 90 stalls, and conversations about how best to use the structure have been underway.

Another existing building fronting the track, and one that has been gutted, is a former dormitory where employees were housed and fed, along with an old blacksmith shop currently used for storage.

A stallion barn, home to Native Dancer, also stands tall but is devoid of life and purpose. Possibilities include repurposing it as a museum to honor Sagamore Farm's most eminent stallions.

The way we see it, in the most resourceful and inspiring ways, Sagamore Farm is an evolving story. Much like owner Kevin Plank— whose Shared Account at a 46/1 shot won the Breeders Cup $2 million Filly and Mare Turf race in 2010, and whose Millionreasonswhy won the Matron in 2011 before coming in second by a neck in the $100,000 Miss Preakness Stakes in 2012— we are just getting started.

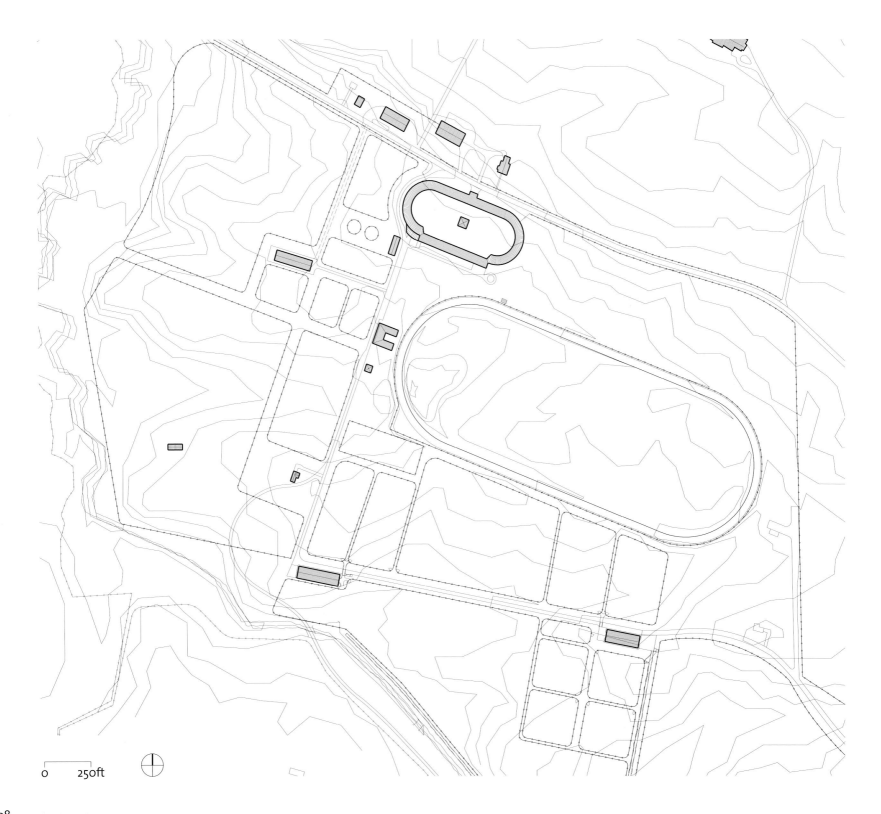

0   250ft

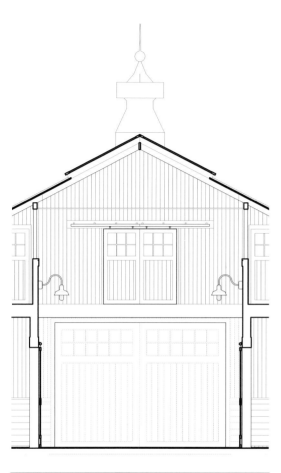

OAKHAVEN FARM
home on the range

As a horse person you will spend a lot of time in the barn, therefore the barn needs to consider the social needs of the equestrian just as it needs to consider the health needs of the horse.

John Blackburn

In the central part of the state, just west of Austin and north of San Antonio, Texas' profoundly hot, dry Hill Country is home to the former Texas White House—the famous LBJ ranch. Noted as well for millennia-old striking limestone and granite rock formations, the region appealed to a horse-loving client, her insurance executive husband, and their young family who'd traded miles of Midwestern malls and amenities for Texas Hill Country's rustic lifestyle and spare, rugged vistas.

Having ridden since childhood, and wanting to introduce her three children to the world of horses, the client and her husband purchased a cattle ranch on 90 acres. Here, she would share in the experience of riding with her two daughters as their own passion for all things equine quickly emerged.

As I'd never been to Austin or Texas Hill Country, the region's vernacular piqued my curiosity. Defined by Texas live oaks, prickly pear cacti, yucca, and stone outcroppings everywhere in this rocky rangeland, I quickly decided it was a beautiful, challenging landscape. My experiences were underscored by a roiling creek bed I had to navigate straight out of a Larry McMurtry novel—and in fact drive straight through— on approach to the homeowners' property (good thing it wasn't rainy season).

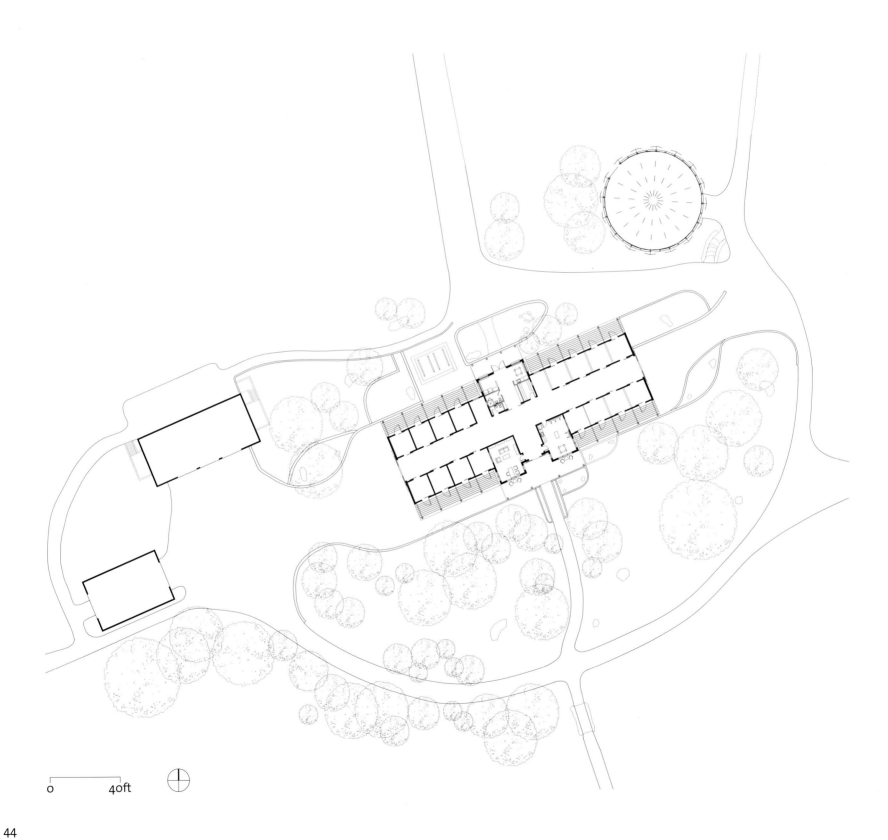

44

While the residence was a long, modest, one-story structure emblematic of the region, its uniqueness was evident in a covered front porch with cedar logs for pillars—something of which I immediately made note. With a barn program that designated a place for the client, her daughters, and their friends to refresh their horses after a brisk ride or long day on the trails, the inclusion of a barn office, tack room, feed and tool rooms, and laundry area were also on the list. A special aspect of the barn in which the homeowner could relax with an iced tea, see her horses in the field or observe her daughters in the arena, was also important. In short, the goal at Oakhaven Farm was multifaceted, and in some ways the barn was to be more social than others I'd designed (or would design) in which training or racing was paramount—a decision based on a thorough investigation of the client's lifestyle. At the same time, though the planned environment was more relaxed, architectural measures ensuring the health and safety of its horses would not be compromised.

All the while mandating a 16-stall structure with an open stall system, the first order of business was to get a couple of Hunter Jumpers onto the property during the master plan and construction processes. To that end, we built a comfortable two-stall barn. In this regard, we were able to use the smaller structure as a kind of test barn in which to incorporate many of the elements and materials considered for the larger one.

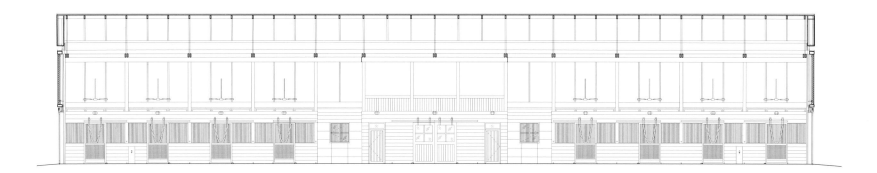

On the open stall front issue, while we typically do not build that way except for foaling barns where constant observation is key, it can be advantageous to do so in a hotter climate such as the one in Texas. While the downside is accumulated bedding in stall corners that can spill out into the aisles, the upside is improved visibility and increased ventilation at all times.

Despite our requisite formula of building barns perpendicular to the prevailing summer breeze to ensure all-important ventilation (Chapter One), Texas Hill Country's rolling land, contouring and uneven elevation issues can preclude a perfect siting. Sometimes, when it comes to topography, we have to ride the horse in the direction he's going. When dealing with rock, it's difficult and costly to alter the landscape, so the goal is to fit the barn to contour.

At Oakhaven, taking into account summer wind direction data, placement of tall trees, rock formations or other obstructions, as well as open fields, seasonal sun orientation and a few additional elements, an assessment of the site's microclimate was possible. The barn's desired orientation was able to be achieved with excellent results.

Imagining the vented skylight, a decision was made to locate it only on the roof's north face. In this case—in a truly hot, parched climate— I was more sensitive to heat build-up than I may have been in more northern venues. Placing the skylight on the north side, we'd have less direct heat build-up, yet bring in the required natural light. We used an 8:12 roof slope to guarantee that the property's extreme heat would be driven up through the ventilated skylight and out, with a 10:12 roof slope for aesthetics at the cross aisle. Industrial cage fans were mounted high on the walls of each stall, allowing the horse to move in and out of the cool draft at will.

Exterior Dutch doors provided for low ventilation in achieving the necessary Bernoulli and chimney effects (Chapter One), where, as in all of our barns, air is brought in low and vented out high—through the skylight. In most cases, Dutch doors offer the added benefit of a visual rhythm to the barn. With a 200-foot-long structure as this one was, an unbroken wall running from end to end is probably not the most aesthetically pleasing design scenario. Accordingly, we took our cues from the residence's bold cedar columns, constructing a perimeter trellis supported by similar posts forged from cedar logs that provided visual continuity.

Seeking to integrate the area's rich, plentiful, characteristic rock into our barn design, a master stonemason, George Salinas—who through family trade and tradition knew the earth and local terrain well—was contracted to help us achieve our goals. In architecture, using stone for an entire building is often exceedingly costly and not always necessary to obtain the desired aesthetic effect. But incorporating stone into a building's low areas, walls, the property's pool area or anything else that can make a statement achieves the objective. Though we used painted standard concrete blocks for the stall walls and heavy timber framing and split-faced, painted concrete masonry block for the exterior side walls of the barn, "Austin stone" was used on the ends—in visually important areas— maintaining a connection with the land.

With a second-story apartment on the back of the barn, the total square footage was brought to 6,674, and as with all of our barns, we did not advocate overhead hay and bedding storage. In this respect, the material becomes a fire hazard, and descending dust and allergens compromise the sensitive respiratory systems of equine residents. In fact, because there is limited rainfall in Texas Hill Country, the client elected to store hay and bedding across a small courtyard in a large service barn without concern about ferrying it back and forth.

Throughout the project, and with an innovative combination hot walker/round pen and additional housing above the service barn part of the farm's master plan, the rugged, natural vernacular of the land and elements informed the design. Special attention was paid to the client's more social program and the horses' health and safety in a severely hot, dry climate. Completed in 2003, in recent years Oakhaven Farm has become more of a breeding operation, its prescient open-stall system conducive to the health, well-being, and safety of the foals.

KETCHEN PLACE FARM
song of the south

We design barns of all types, high

end to very basic. A healthy barn

does not necessarily require high

end finishes. I never had a horse

ask for oak paneled tack rooms

or heavy timber framing.

John Blackburn

Raised in small town Tennessee and attending architecture school at South Carolina's Clemson University, clearly I'm no stranger to the rural South. But despite its sweeping magnolia trees and formidable history, articulated in part by its architecture and enduring family legacies, I was surprised by what I observed on the drive from the airport to a site survey for one of our projected barns at Ketchen Place Farm.

A virtual pocket of poverty with rusting trailers, listing shacks, tattered lean-to's, and jerry-rigged porches that provide little relief from the region's relentless heat and humidity, South Carolina's York County is imbued with a strong Southern heritage nevertheless. Once home to the powerful Catawba Indian Nation, legions of hardy farmers—including dairy farmers from whom Ketchen Place Farm's

current owners are descended—tilled the soil and cultivated crops to feed their cattle. Initially a 200-plus-acre parcel, Ketchen Place Farm was one of a handful of York County dairy farms.

In the years preceding the Civil War, the land entered the current owners' historical purview when landholder Dr. William Ardrey sold it to the Garison family. A Garison descendent subsequently married Adolphus Augustus Theodore Moore Neely, who had a son, A.T. Neely, and daughter, Vivian Lee Neely Ketchen (1888–1957), the latter of whom was the farm's namesake. Currently alive on 30 of its 200 acres, for decades the farm was used for crops to sustain cows though allowed to become fallow when the family's Snow White Dairy bowed to cooperatives and modern production.

Because of its strong Southern sense of place and materials, the extraordinary work of architect Samuel Mockbee and his Auburn University-based Rural Studio came to mind for me in designing the barn at Ketchen Place Farm. A Mississippian by birth, before his untimely death in 2001, the highly decorated Mockbee created an iconic style of community architecture based on his connection with rural Southern life and its hardscrabble populace. Influenced by Mockbee's design philosophy and exercising my own penchant for contextual design, along with a limited budget, I identified simple forms and basic, local materials such as abundant Southern yellow pine and concrete block with corrugated metal roof, to create a shed row-style barn for Ketchen Place Farm. The open post and beam structure was something the clients mandated and is particularly well-suited to warmer climates.

Emblematic of their solid dairymen stock and certainly no strangers to hard work, owners/sisters Mary Carolyn Quarles and Virginia Palmer had first built a rudimentary 82-by-24-foot 7-stall shed row-type barn on the property in 2000—without power tools and with their own hands. A hand auger belonging to their grandfather was used for bolt holes. But following its completion, and because there were 20 horses and about one-third the number of stalls, feeding had to be done in shifts. Due to its size, not all the animals were able to benefit from the structure's minimal protection in bad weather, though in winter they were blanketed appropriately. In fact prior to the sisters' early barn, the horses lived entirely outdoors, as they do in nature (see Preface), with trees providing a little shade in summer and some semblance of protection in winter. All in all it was clearly time to upgrade, especially as the family breeds and sells horses with prospective customers traversing the property. This function of the farm was of particular importance as it was the catalyst for a gracious courtyard design.

As clients, the industrious Mary and Virginia— who had ridden in exchange for stable work since they were young girls— were very hands-on in the planning and execution of the new barn. Along with their septuagenarian mother, Peggy Palmer, who also lives on the property, they were and still are the barn's entire staff. With Virginia working as an engineer by day, the brunt of the work typically falls to Mary (with her Clemson University degree in animal industries). Accordingly, a functional, durable, no-frills, easily maintainable barn was our

goal, without compromising our formula for natural light and ventilation though it would need to be modified somewhat. At 10,613 square feet, the barn needed to stable all 20 horses—stallions, broodmares, thoroughbreds off the racetrack who have become sport horses, and Warmbloods—all used primarily for student training and breeding.

Though our typical modus operandi is to build a large center aisle barn with a vented, ridge skylight and ventilation lower to the ground as well, sited perpendicular to the prevailing summer breeze, the health and safety issues of a less costly shed row-style barn are the same—never subordinated to design, finishes, or other materials. But the shape of the structure is naturally quite different.

Arranged around the courtyard, the shed row in and of itself did not fit our typical design philosophy for optimal Bernoulli-type ventilation (see Heronwood Farm). But having produced other barns in the state around Aiken and Camden, I'd had the opportunity to observe popular turn-of-the-century courtyard-style barns, nevertheless; as such the design for Ketchen Place Farm fit easily into the area's historic equestrian context.

At construction, we were able to site the open end of the courtyard itself perpendicular to the prevailing summer breeze so the air would hit it at somewhat of an angle, enter the barn, and climb the interior slope of the roof which was vented by louvers. In that way ventilation was achieved, and in short we were able to arrange the courtyard, shed row barn, and paddocks so that they captured the summer wind from across the surrounding fields. While some may assume an open-style barn

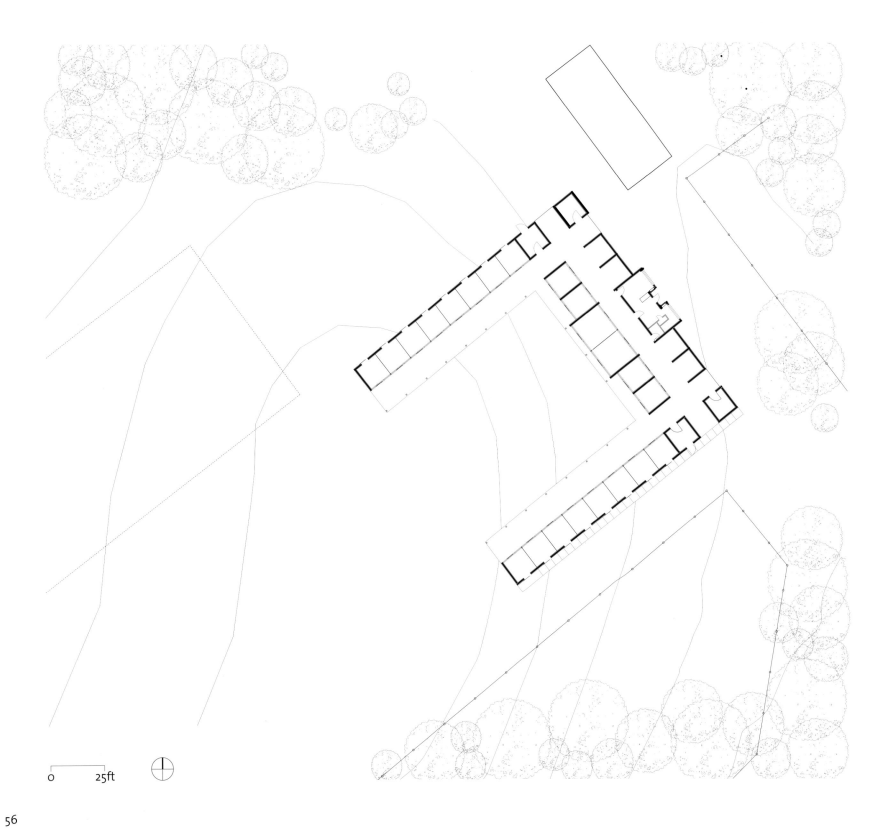

naturally ventilates on its own, our objective is more proactive in that we labor to move air, heat, and humidity up and out, creating a circulating, cooling effect by design. On an aesthetic note, the courtyard also opened to the property's entrance.

Where light is concerned, because this style of barn is only one stall deep, it is predisposed to natural illumination. Creating a translucent, vented clerestory window across the very top of the front of the stalls that rose to the rafters further courted natural light. Additionally, we used the roof with its 4:12 slope (2:12 over the aisle) as an umbrella. Open underneath and at the eaves, with additional ventilation achieved by incorporating full louvers at the ends of the stalls, any heated air that may start to accumulate would tend to vent out quickly

above the clerestory and not become trapped to affect the stalls. On the back side of the stalls Dutch doors also let in light and air, as do sliding doors in the front. Fans located high in each stall always allow the horse to go in and out of the breeze as desired.

Paying homage to Mockbee's Rural Studio which emphasizes use of local materials, stained and painted Southern yellow pine—prolific in the region—frames the barn's roof, which is made of heavy gauge corrugated metal. Walls are concrete block masonry. Eschewing fancy paneling like the oak that might be seen in other barns, the structure stands firm in its South Carolina vernacular. An air-conditioned loft space with full view of the foaling stalls was also constructed in the barn so that Virginia, who lives off-property,

can remain close during foaling. A projected service building, to be located parallel to the barn, will house farm vehicles and the like. As Mary and Virginia's out-of-state Uncle William Edward Senn is a prominent member of the family, and commissioned the barn with his nieces, a second level two-bedroom apartment in the service building is planned for his visits.

Overall our objective was to use basic, local materials to articulate the design while making it as aesthetically pleasing in its detail as it is simple and functional. Exemplary of its neighborhood and the owners' particular needs, and inspired by Sam Mockbee's contextual tenets, Ketchen Place Farm is a simple architectural paean to the rural South.

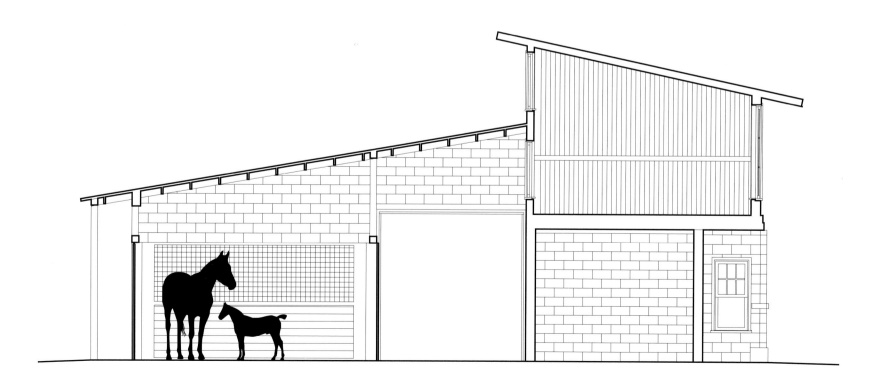

DEVINE RANCH
california dreamin'

You can cut corners to save on construction costs only to spend any savings and more in inefficient operation. Good design must balance both.

John Blackburn

Go West, young man, or middle-aged architect as the case happened to be. Certainly by 2002 the technology to largely design and execute a project in a dotcom world had precluded the concept of geography as a negative. Delivery and distance had dissolved into software and Skype. Subsequently, I received a call in D.C. from a Silicon Valley businessman to do an initial site visit on 80 acres. The objective was a residence and horse ranch in Aptos, California.

Located in Santa Cruz County near the San Andreas Fault, rural Aptos with its rolling hills was home to a booming redwood timber harvesting industry in the late 19th and early 20th centuries. When the hills were stripped bare circa 1960, the region became agricultural, defined by vast orchards, vineyards, artichokes, lettuce, and more. It was this kind of sensitivity and deference to the land that influenced the owner's sensibilities for the

projected Devine Ranch. In short, he wanted to build a residence, service facility, and other buildings, and a safe, healthy barn for his wife's and daughter's horses, who rode Western and English, respectively. The goal was to do this without stripping the land of its orchards and vineyards—something which may also have raised the concern and even the ire of neighboring agronomists.

Commissioned to do a master plan for the property, the client's initial program called for a small service building for hay bedding and storage and to house his hobbies that included RV'ing and sculling, with a couple of basic horse stalls as well. This structure was to be built at the bottom of a hill among the orchards to confine storage to one area and not pepper the hilltop with structures

that might obstruct the view. It was also to be small in scale so as not to decimate the landscape with extensive construction. A larger, primary barn was to be sited about 100 feet up at the top of the hill, along with the residence, where the terrain was previously given to grazing, rather than farming. In this respect there would be minimal incursion into any agriculture up there.

As the fates would have it, and as construction moved forward, the client decided to build out the footprint of the smaller, bottom of the hill facility, where it would become the primary 8-stall 2,270-square-foot barn. Where our Eastern barns commonly involve dormers and cupolas, in Aptos the client opted for a

more Western Tahoe-style look: heavy timber columns and a stone base, which we would also use on the residence.

As the service building's foundation had been laid and construction begun prior to designating it as the main barn, we did not have the opportunity to site it precisely perpendicular to the prevailing summer breeze. The region, though arid, does receive Monterrey Bay and Pacific Ocean breezes. We were also confronting a long, narrow site identified primarily for service vehicles at first, hence its less-than-perfect orientation. Where the roof was concerned, we were able to build an 8:12 slope which would help with ventilation, as would exterior Dutch doors on each stall where the client also mandated turnout spaces for the animals' independence of movement.

Built as a center-aisle barn, unlike many in California which are shed row due to temperate weather year round, Devine Ranch's stalls are located primarily on one side of the barn. An office, tack room, wash stall, laundry room and storage, and two additional stalls are located on the other. A continuous ridge skylight, vented at both the top and bottom and running the length of the roof, provides for optimal heat and air management and natural light. Additionally, yoke gates allow the horses to look out—essentially for some equine surveillance, so to speak (see Preface)—when confined to their stalls.

As horses are flight animals, the option to look around in response to an unfamiliar sound and see their handlers, observe calmness, and whatever else they may need to reassure them is just good stable management. Yoke gates are also especially important at Devine Ranch as the inter-stall walls are solid so there is no interaction between the horses. Many times we will carve open spaces into dividing walls, but in that Aptos is an earthquake zone—in fact it is close to the epicenter of the 1989 Loma Prieta quake (my very first shaker was experienced onsite)—solid walls were needed to help fortify the entire structure.

Early on, the family desired a barn that would accommodate both Western and English riding accoutrements, but in the end the design was simplified to conform to only Western requisites. While the client was partial to California Redwood, in a nod to preservation, cedar was chosen for barn and residence siding and for other ranch buildings that followed. Framing was structured with Douglas fir. In fact, many of the materials chosen for the smaller barn—Douglas fir framing; cedar

siding; wood stain; skylight and window frames; skylight tint—were done so as a test for the impending, larger barn, into which the smaller barn evolved. Even the mortar and the manner in which the stone was laid were tested on the initial structure before we got to the large barn and residence.

During construction, as the decision was made to transform the previously designated (smaller) service building into the primary barn, overcoming issues created by the open web trusses we'd already installed was a challenge. Trusses are generally not recommended in our horse barn designs as they accumulate layers of dust, cobwebs, birds' nests and more—all potential purveyors of allergens, pathogens, and bacteria which may compromise an equine's sensitive respiratory system and also create fire hazards. Frequent vacuuming, though challenging at that height, can minimize risk.

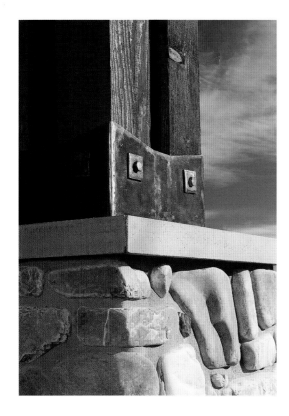

As with all of our barns, storing hay and bedding overhead—one of the leading causes of respiratory illness and barn fires—was vetoed. A dividing wall separates the rest of the barn from a storage area for daily use, with bulk hay and bedding confined to a separate facility on the north end of the property.

To complement the barn, the 7,000-square-foot post-and-beam residence on top of the hill with its copper gutters and fieldstone also has heavy timber columns and a stone base, along with projecting overhang and additional use of timber in its rafter tails. It has distant views of Monterrey Bay, and the owner's views of an agriculturally-minded horse farm were fully realized.

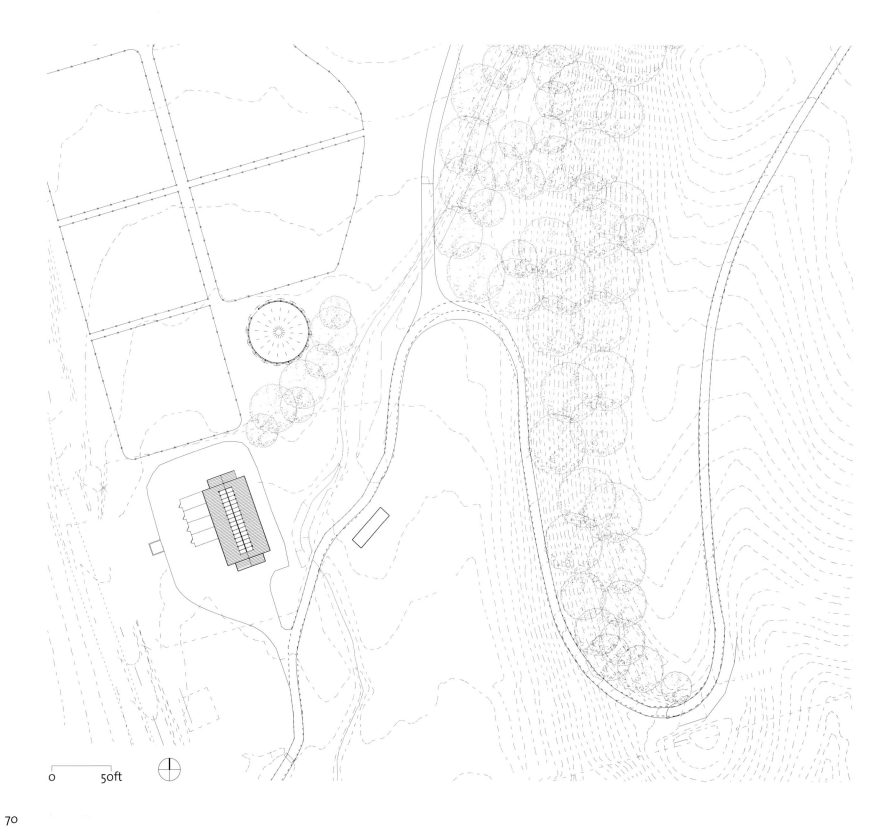

0   50ft

LUCKY JACK FARM
a place in the sun

*A successful equestrian design requires
a balance to the demands of the site,
the goals of the owner, and the needs
of the horse but with the needs of the
horse remaining a priority.*

Author unknown

In our quest to design Lucky Jack Farm in Rancho Santa Fe, California, we were confronted by a plethora of code, architectural, municipal, county, environmental, programmatic, and geological challenges and restrictions. Though accustomed to a variety of issues that often challenge our efforts to articulate the health and safety of horses through design, each and every site is different. In fact, some are quite unique, such as a regional aqueduct located on this steep, sprawling Rancho Santa Fe property. Nevertheless we were prepared to work, in part facilitated by local California architect Allard Jansen who helped us navigate the local terrain, both literally and figuratively.

In the end, the complicated design (and multiple redesign) process resulted in a dramatic, singular outcome. Most would agree the final Lucky Jack Farm project is as much a tribute to architecture and aesthetics as it is to location and environment.
To paraphrase a popular adage, we turned obstacles and restrictions into lemonade.

Seeking a barn for her own Hunter Jumper horses, a trainer, and somewhere friends would be invited to board their animals, the client also wanted a clubhouse/entertainment center with inspired kitchen and guest quarters where her husband and family, who did not ride, and their equestrian and non-equestrian friends could gather throughout the day or evening. In this regard, the client's love of riding and time-consuming barn-related responsibilities would not serve to isolate her from other important components of her life.

Because architecturally controlled Rancho Santa Fe was developed by renowned architect Lilian Rice in the 1920s and has an historic designation, a rather intractable design code, characterized by low-slung terra cotta roofs, shuttered, deep-set windows, white or neutral-colored adobe walls, and intimate patios and courtyards, defines the area. Today it is known

as California Romantica, California Mission or Spanish Colonial style. In this case, the owner had chosen a property just outside the historic district, so while we weren't bound by mandated design parameters, we did want to honor the style. As the health and safety of horses is always paramount in our work, we chose to trim our design sails accordingly.

Tantamount to all that, with the client identifying a site in what San Diego County considers a wildlife interface area, also home to endangered species, and in light of the state's stringent wildfire zoning and building restrictions, our tests mounted. The site also sloped about 240 feet from top to bottom providing serious construction challenges as well as safety concerns for the horses.

Upon arrival at the site, a deteriorated equestrian facility with vacant and rusted prefabricated barn and small ranch-style house greeted us. The barn sat at the lower end of the property with the residence perched about 60 feet above it. With initial thoughts of preserving and renovating a portion of the house for guests or a tenant, the client also wanted to tear down the barn and build another precisely on the existing pad. What made more sense, however, was to locate the barn up where the house was, facing west, due to better ventilation thanks to the constant Pacific Ocean winds cooling the site. In short, the barn would breathe better at a higher elevation on the property. We also decided to raze the house and construct the clubhouse on the same level, near the barn. And because of zoning issues we were allowed only 4,000 square feet for the 16-stall barn, deemed an accessory structure, so we decided to locate the tack room inside the clubhouse where square footage was not limited. Wash and grooming stalls were built under a shed structure separate but parallel to the barn.

Integral to Lucky Jack Farm's design was a courtyard—redolent of Rancho Santa Fe's Lilian Rice architectural style, framed by a trellis that visually connects the barn and clubhouse. In fact one of my great concerns at this juncture in building a courtyard to be utilized by horses, as well as people, was that there was a considerable drop-off along the western edge. There would be a safety risk involved if a horse got loose, so we mitigated this issue with the unobtrusive use of the trellis as a barrier, fencing, and landscaping which, while aesthetically pleasing, all serve as visual and

physical boundaries. On warm afternoons the courtyard and its assets also provide welcome shade and a terrace respite, inviting visitors to take in the view of the Pacific Ocean.

Where the barn itself was concerned, while we typically elect to do an 7:12 minimum roof slope to create the chimney and Bernoulli effects we seek in all of our barns (see Heronwood Farm), once again architectural style mandates for the area identified a lower pitch—even something like a 3:12. While the property was outside the historical district and we were not bound by this, we still wanted it reflected in our buildings. Ultimately we compromised on a 6:12 slope,

which, while not perfect for airflow purposes, was nevertheless acceptable due to the site's exposure to sweeping Pacific Ocean breezes.

We also used terra cotta tiles which both reflected the Lilian Rice style of architecture and in this case would serve to insulate the roof from baking sun on days where there was no wind. With a steep roof, which is what we generally prescribe, penetrating heat catalyzes the chimney and Bernoulli effects, but not so with Lucky Jack's lower slope. Subsequently terra cotta was an agreeable solution. Dutch doors on the exterior of the stalls also facilitated ventilation and would provide quick egress in an emergency.

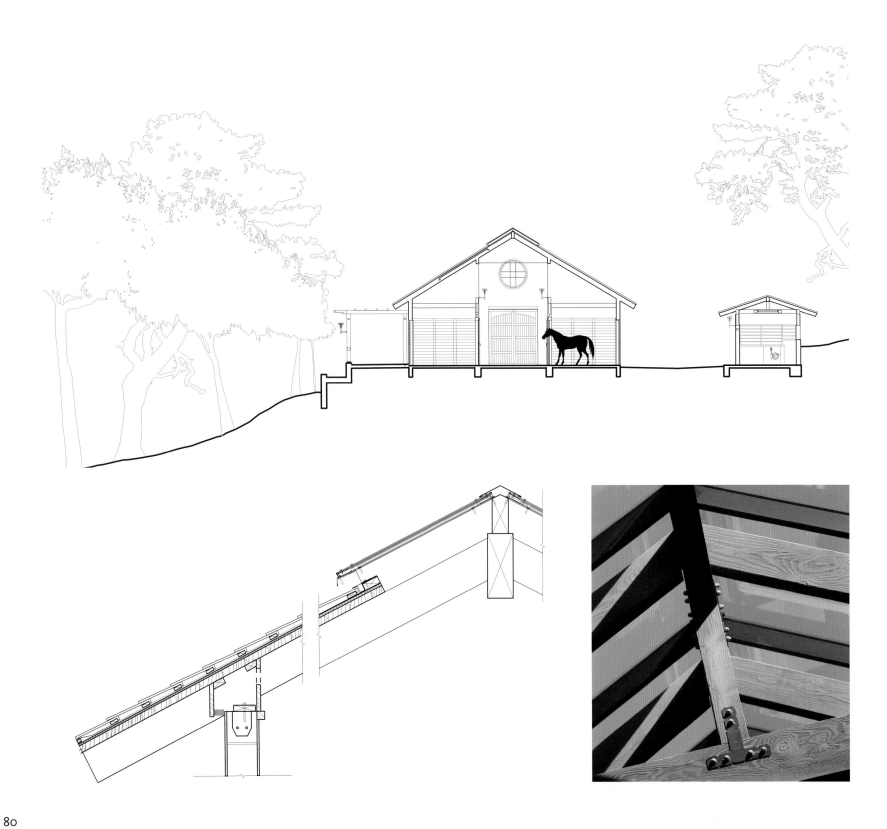

With the aforementioned stringent code requirements that accrue to this wildfire region, we could not vent the barn's eaves as we often do because of the possibility of embers being drawn through openings. Accordingly, we vented high at the roof where the ridge skylight sits and the openings would be much smaller. At most farms we use a polycarbonate skylight material which diffuses harsh sunlight, but wildlife code issues at Lucky Jack Farm precluded the material as it was deemed not durable enough. We initially decided on a stronger tempered glass but discovered that it was still not sufficient as the code dictated that we use screening underneath to catch any shards if it broke. Screening in itself is a fire hazard for barns as birds, bird nests, feathers, droppings, cobwebs, and other combustible materials accumulate, however. Ultimately, we went with safety glass for the 90-foot skylight, which, while not absolutely indestructible, came close enough to satisfy the powers that be.

Additionally, and again because we could not vent at the eaves, we used a skylight with a system we'd developed using a perforated Z-channel which fosters ventilation. The perforations hug the underside of the skylight which prevents snow (not an issue in this area of the country) and rain from entering for the most part, though an ideal horse barn environment imitates nature so these elements would not be foreign to equine residents.

Perforated in the right ratio from the top down, these openings are only about $\frac{1}{16}$ of an inch in size precluding embers from a wildfire entering the barn that way (maximum size for an opening, per code, is $\frac{1}{4}$ inch). Aesthetically, when additional roof or eaves vents are not possible,

a perforated Z-channel skylight is preferable as its streamlined design creates a floating effect for the polycarbonate or glass skylight, producing a nice shadow line as well.

Facing extensive geological issues, when we went to build the round pen we confronted a 130-foot easement on the property which essentially bisected the steep site in two, with three 60-to-90-inch diameter underground pipes that affected how much we could disturb the ground above. Functioning as an aqueduct for this area, restrictions mounted, as anything placed within the easement's parameters had to be built to be taken apart if the aqueduct ever needed servicing and the round pen was built accordingly. The round pen's location also called for site grading, though for conservation purposes the county regulation limits the amount of earth that can be disturbed to 2,000 cubic yards for a minor grading permit, which was desired. Moving dirt offsite or trucking in new dirt is expensive and produces more emissions while consuming significant amounts of energy. Also, applying for a major grading permit, which wasn't really necessary, would have required additional time and expense, delaying construction.

We also left the top portion of the property above the easement undisturbed as the California Gnatcatcher (*Polioptila Californica*), seeking "Critical Habitat" designation under the Endangered Species Act pending court review at the time, populates Lucky Jack's crest.

The 3,900-square-foot timber-framed clubhouse and guest suite building has a terra cotta roof, in deference to Lilian Rice-style architecture,

though we used flat-style terra cotta as opposed to the historical district-mandated curve barrel shape. An outdoor fireplace and high end finishes including marble countertops and marble tile backsplash, faux stucco walls, and Douglas fir wood flooring make the space functional and elegant. A 5.2 kilowatt solar photovoltaic array was installed to reduce energy consumption and also expedite the permitting process due to California's Green Building Initiative.

Because we prefer to avoid the idea of overhead hay and bedding storage in all of our barns due to the increased fire risk and the opportunity for allergens, pathogens, and bacteria to irritate horses' sensitive respiratory

systems, a storage facility for these items and vehicles was located in a separate structure on the site, with 5-to-7-day storage within the barn itself (although not overhead). With a dry, temperate climate that includes little rain, transporting fresh hay and bedding to the barn once a week or so was not an issue.

For Lucky Jack Farm we were clearly compelled to look at our plans through multiple lenses time and time again. Despite the stringent review process we never lost sight of what works best for the health and safety of horses, and with that the unique challenges set before us ultimately forged the design.

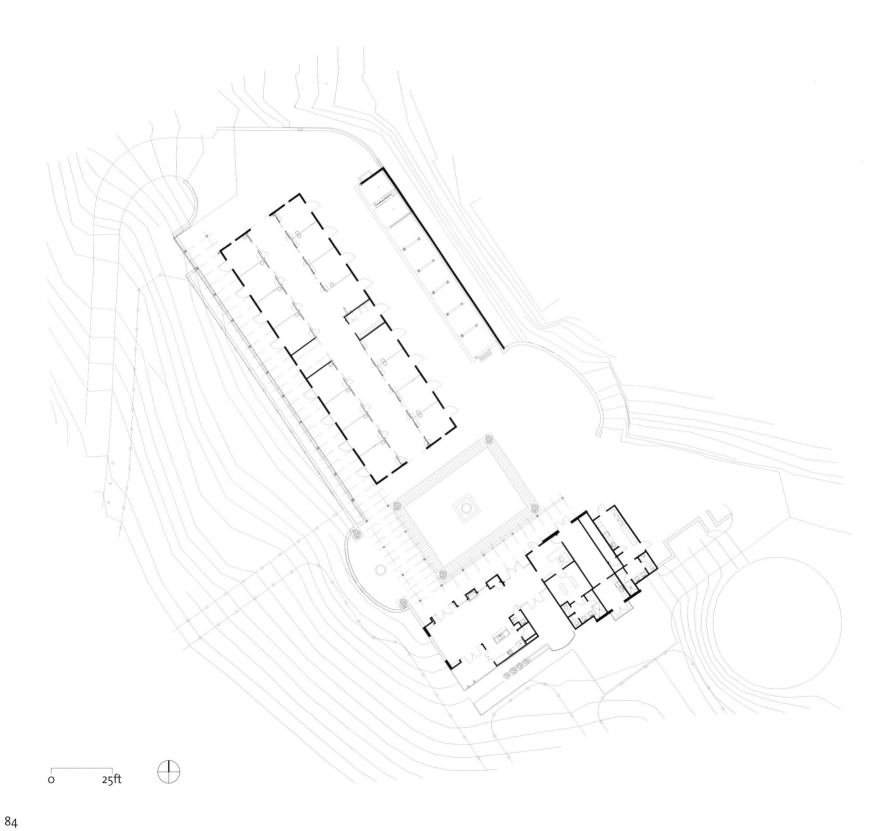

0 25ft

84

RIVER FARM
a family affair

I was asked once to describe the ultimate barn and I've been searching for that answer for 30 years. There is no ultimate barn. Every site, client, and horse is different; no one barn fits all.

John Blackburn

Desiring a farm on 200 largely river-view acres, a Virginia entrepreneur with ties to the Washington Capitals and Nationals teams wanted a distinctive, family-oriented compound. The goal was an enclave where he, his equestrian wife and their children, horses, cattle, and members of an extended family—some of whom would manage the farm—could make their respective homes.

Seeking a 20-stall barn, arena, service building, and several family residences (which we did not design) just north of Leesburg, space abounded and consisted of rolling pastures, woods, and a bluff that sits approximately 60 or 70 feet above the Potomac River. The property continued to rise to a high point near the center of the farm where the original homestead was located. The projected horse

barn for this spectacular site was to house their animals and board invited guests' horses, and perhaps a trainer, as their accomplished young daughter was on course to ride competitively.

Presumably a functioning farmstead at the time of the Civil War, an original bank barn on the property—a style of barn where part of the lower portion is built into a hillside, something endemic to the Mid-Atlantic region—also became one of our projects. Though the original barn structure may not have survived the Civil War in this embattled area, we surmised its foundation may have predated it. Because the client's wife had considerable environmental concerns and had adopted green practices, much of our site design was driven by these factors, including our goal for the bank barn, which was to preserve as much of the severely deteriorating historic structure as possible.

An existing adjacent corn crib constructed without foundations was removed, rebuilt, and transformed into a sundeck with a southwest exposure, with the bank barn's northeast façade replaced with floor-to-ceiling glass. Clad this time in board-and-batten skin and garnering panoramic Potomac River views through the glass, the bank barn became a sparkling social center for family and friends, winning various architecture and media awards in historic resources and restoration.

Where the horse barn was concerned, as always, our primary goal was promoting the health and safety of horses while responding to the environment. In this case, we sited the barn closer to the entrance road to keep the rest of the property more discrete. As a family compound, privacy for its residents was key in light of the comings and goings

of employees, service personnel, and others. The property also backed up to the river, which would be designated for residences and overall family use.

Given the high point in the middle of the property, we were faced with a decision to build on either the north or south side. The latter was where the land sloped the most so we chose that orientation. It allowed us to site the barn and arena using natural terrain as much as possible, in order to push the arena down into the natural slope of the hill, which in turn keeps the scale down.

Under flat conditions the ridge of the arena would be significantly higher than the barn and by lowering the arena floor by as much as 6 feet, and providing an enclosed ramp for access from the barn, we were able to visually reduce the scale of the arena relative to the barn. This allowed the public entrance at the observation room to be elevated to align with the top of the kick wall.

Our preference for optimal ventilation and prevention of the spread of disease is to site the barn perpendicular to the prevailing summer breeze (see Heronwood Farm). At River Farm, the slope of the land and existing vegetation—which impact the microclimate of the site—allowed us to position the barn and arena in an ideal manner to solve a host of issues that not only include ventilation but also site drainage and the aforementioned arena height issue.

Also affecting barn siting was a matter of aesthetics: how the barn would be seen from the home site. We did, as always, investigate local wind patterns and location of trees, so in the end we weren't too far off. The prevailing summer breeze is from the southwest, and the barn faces slightly more west. The arena, which is perpendicular though connected to the barn, was featured further downhill, with its long roof oriented south to prepare for photovoltaic panels as they were part of the discussion at the outset.

A series of shed dormers, though poised for aesthetics, were also integral to the barn's light and ventilation. At River Farm the typical ridge skylight was relegated to a left—or west— side skylight only, as the client desired that it was not visible from the residences. With dormers on the right, or east, a balance of light and air was subsequently achieved— additional venting attained through a break in the roof running along the edge of the dormers. An 8:12 roof slope further facilitated the desired Bernoulli effect (see Heronwood Farm), as did exterior Dutch doors for venting in low.

Because of the 20-stall layout, the barn was designed in a symmetrical style which is the most efficient for barns with 20 or more stalls. With service elements including two grooming stalls and two wash stalls in the center portion, family horses could be stabled at one end with boarders at the other. In fact, a divider wall at the end of the stalls is actually a masonry firewall, separating the horses from the center, followed by an enclosed ramp to the arena.

In the event of an emergency, with doors closed, the center portion with its masonry wall is designed to slow the migration of smoke and fire so horses have a better chance of being successfully removed from the structure. To this end, and to facilitate overall operation, the barn also has a wider than average center aisle—about 20 feet in width—giving animals and workers a wide berth in their daily activities (gone are the ubiquitous cross-tie issues that hinder routine in so many barns, as these are typically located in the center wash/grooming section).

Using interlocking rubber brick flooring throughout the center aisle, the center portion also reaps the benefits of radiant heat in the winter. This provides comfort for workers, something more likely to be instituted in a sport training or recreational barn than a thoroughbred facility. Except for grooming, horses remain in other parts of the barn in cooler, more equine-suitable temperatures where the natural climate is encouraged rather than mitigated as the best environment for a horse is one that mimics nature. An isolation stall was also created in the center for sick or injured horses, more readily used for seven-day storage of hay and bedding.

Once again at this farm we used yoke gates. These allow the horse an at-will view of comings and goings up and down the aisle, providing them with peace of mind and better mental health—less anxiety in light of unfamiliar noises and occurrences they may wish to visually investigate (see Preface). Though the aisle of walls between the stalls is relatively open, employing bars, solid panels along feed buckets are a stress-relieving detail. Without them, a dominant animal in a stall next to another may be perceived as a threat by the latter, whereby he may decline from

approaching his own food and water. A 4-foot panel provides a visual barrier between the two stalls and though we did not invent the practice, it is strongly recommended in our barns without solid dividing walls. Also at River Farm, feed buckets were built into small cabinets accessed from the center aisle, cabinets which also store boots, wraps, and anything else one might require for interaction with the horse without having to sacrifice time traipsing back to the tack room.

A unique aspect of River Farm's main barn is that on the west side, stalls have their own turnouts measuring about the width of the stall and two stall lengths long: 12-by-24 feet. A series of swing gates open to allow the animal to go from stall to turnout to paddock and back. In this respect, the horse has more freedom and control over his environment and busy workers can allocate their time to other important tasks. This system does not exist on the barn's east, or front, side for aesthetic reasons, as the grounds are fully landscaped and more visible from residences.

Also inside, a large loft-style office with a lounge/kitchen was created, intended initially for the client, who does not ride, to have his own space while being a part of his wife and daughter's equine pursuits. This space has since become the farm office, overlooking the center wash/grooming area and with an unobstructed view down the center aisle.

As mentioned, the 25,000-square-foot indoor arena sits lower than the barn— by essentially 6 feet—and is accessed by an enclosed ramp, albeit with sliding double doors on both sides of the barn. The barn is the structure that dominates the landscape, as many

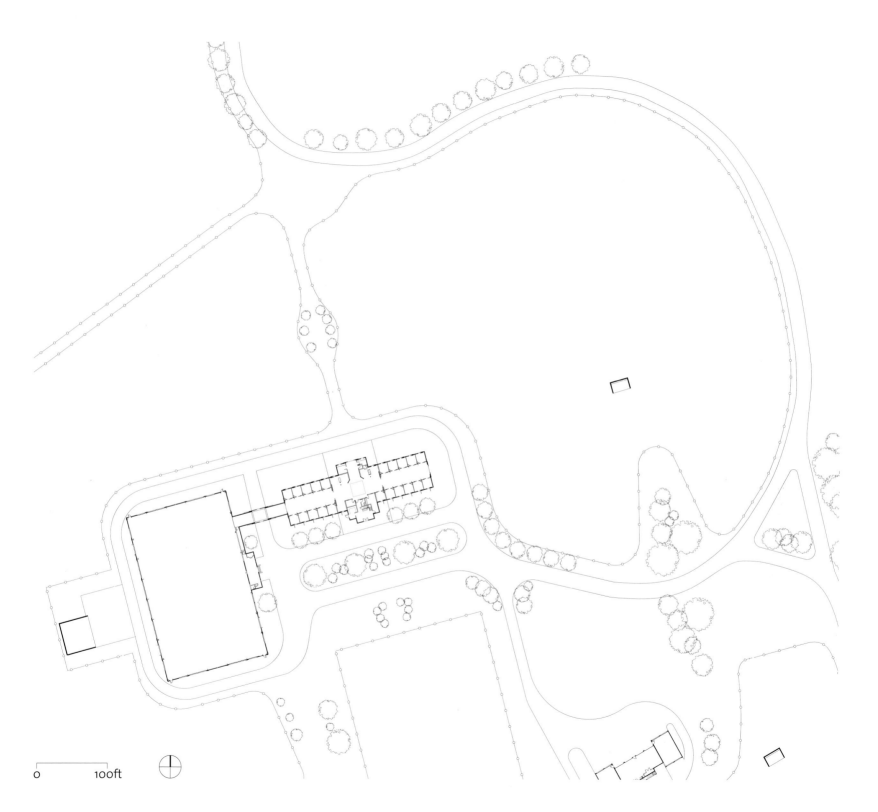

0   100ft

River Farm   95

arenas resemble unattractive airplane hangars planted in one's back yard. Additionally, unlike most arenas, here someone does not have to climb a series of steps to traverse the kick wall and enter the observation area. The arena contains 34 roll-up and 4 stationary doors, along with considerable concealed storage space easily accessed. Because of the arena skylight and other natural light factors, family and observers have noted there isn't a single dark spot at any time, which was certainly our goal.

Furnished much like a living room with couches and other plush seating, the observation area also boasts a kitchen and restroom. Its open concept was created for people to sit and relax, cook a meal or prepare some treats, and watch the game on a flat screen television if desired, all while viewing the riders. Rustic chandeliers in the observation room, barn, and aisle add an uncommon aesthetic.

Where the connecting ramp is concerned, massive sliding double doors on either side provide another element of safety for horses in the event of fire. In this sense, a fire truck could drive or haul hoses directly into the barn and/or through to the other side without having to circumnavigate the entire barn to get from one end to the other. Farm vehicles can also transport hay, bedding, and almost anything else into the barn this way without having to turn around or back up.

Strategic placement of storage and service buildings—one with a staff apartment—break up the scale of the property so that it resembles a friendly village, with service vehicles routed so as not to affect the environment and remain on the periphery of the farm. Horses, vehicles, and

the public come together at the right locations but do not have to cross. If there is a party or other special event planned for the historical bank barn, the sundeck-topped corn crib has a ground level access to storage that can be used to store trays of food, additional chairs, tables, and just about anything else so no one has to look out and see catering vehicles or party trucks and gear parked and spread out front or even to the side.

Emblematic of a real lifestyle choice for a close, extended family, River Farm is also a strong manifestation of our efforts to design for the health and safety of horses. Built as much as possible in deference to the environment, and with an eye to preserving the site's historic elements, the barn and compound stand as a solid example of our work.

BEECHWOOD STABLES

when the cold wind blows

The investment in your barn needs to

reflect the investment in your horse.

The barn is a reflection of your concern

and the value you have for him.

John Blackburn

While New England didn't exactly invent winter, living in a region beset by frigid winds, ice storms, and a foot or two of snow accumulating on any given day is a challenge for both humans and animals.

What's more when you combine weather considerations with an area steeped in history, along with site restrictions and an Architectural Access Board that subscribes to a strict, literal interpretation of the Americans with Disabilities Act (ADA) even for a horse barn, which sometimes proved dichotomous to ensuring the health and safety of horses, the formula for success is challenging at best.

At the project's inception, the client had obtained a site less than a mile from the family's residence—the property itself

formerly a group of athletic fields belonging to a private school which had purchased the old Leadbetter Farm dating back to the late 1700s or early 1800s. Historic buildings still standing included an old farmhouse and bank barn that had apparently weathered its share of storms and had been modified many times with additions and "modernizations," though they were not of practical use for the current owner's needs.

Early on the primary problem for all concerned was that the land area was quite limited—not enough space for the projected 8,300-square-foot, 12-stall Hunter Jumper barn, arenas (indoor and outdoor), paddock, and service buildings the client wanted. There were also restrictions in the region with numerous jurisdictional and code requirements affecting the site plan, runoff, and more, and potential community concerns as we were now taking this historic property and transforming it into a horse farm. Eventually some land next door was acquired, increasing the farm to 11 acres, and we embarked on a long road of the aforementioned challenges.

While issues of handicap accessibility have always been paramount in other aspects of our practice designing residential, commercial, and institutional projects, and we've certainly implemented measures at other farms particularly in heavy public-access spaces such as the observation areas of arenas, Beechwood Stables set a precedent for us in a proposed horse barn. In this case, ADA requirements included such devices as wheelchair-accessible horse stalls. In response we explained that it was unacceptable for an individual to enter a stall in a wheelchair with a 1,500-pound

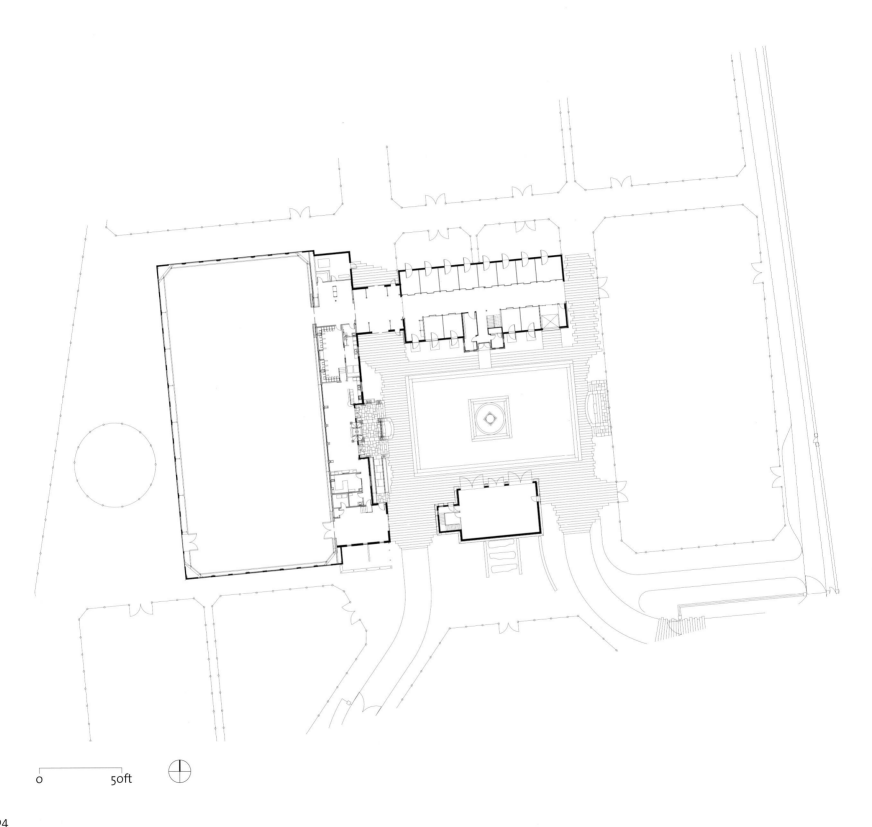

0   50ft

animal, placing that individual at risk, and compromising the safety and well-being of the horse as well.

Another ADA-proposed action was for us to add an electric button-operated release on aisle doors. Seasoned horse owners know that equines are highly intelligent creatures, and it wouldn't take much for an observant horse to learn to operate the exit button and let himself out—a huge safety risk. Clearly horses learn by watching and habit. In the end, handicap-accessible elements such as a ramp that facilitated access to the arena's observation area were made, as well as handicap-accessible restrooms in two locations within the arena. All of the non-barn and non-stall doors were outfitted with ADA-approved operating hardware and closers, but for the safety of both humans and equines alike we did not alter our plan for the barn and stalls.

Based on a New England style of architecture, a considerable amount of locally sourced heavy timber was used to frame the barn, the arena, and the observation area. Stonework including a custom stone fireplace afforded a ski lodge-type presence to the arena, something the client mandated. This type of aesthetic provides a focal point and strengthens the social amenities of the observation room as a place for owners, trainers, and invited guests to relax in winter, as does the enhanced courtyard space in milder seasons. Working with locals Marcus Gleysteen Architects, landscape architect Gregory Lombardi Design, and interior designer SLC Interiors, the team produced a landscaped entrance court, heavy timber-framed entry terrace, and observation room. There were two fireplaces back to back—one in the observation room and one in the outdoor terrace—as well as a custom millwork-designed tack room.

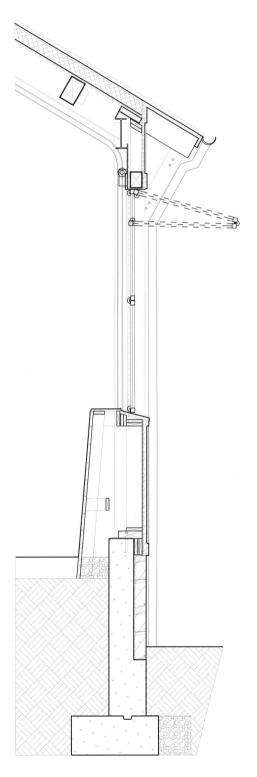

Because of the harsh New England winters, the client opted for an overhead hayloft rather than traipsing back and forth to a separate storage facility. We did, nevertheless, leave the hayloft open so as not to impede natural light and ventilation. In fact the hayloft serves to keep some of the horses' body heat inside the barn in winter. Conversely while an overhead hayloft is something we typically do not advocate as allergens, pathogens, and bacteria from hay particles can impact horses' sensitive respiratory systems and pose a serious fire risk, the barn was equipped with a prolific sprinkler system. Interestingly, heavy timber is also more durable and fire-resistant than steel, so even with the overhead hayloft this barn focuses on fire safety through its materials and systems. And the former is a better insulator than steel in northern climes.

For aesthetics, where we'd traditionally use a concrete border to flank the center aisle with its interlocking rubber brick, the client took the stone work concept one step further by using a 12-to-14-inch granite border. The thresholds of each stall are also granite, and four-sided granite plinths support the barn's columns. Chamfered edges make these columns safer for the horses.

Where ventilation is concerned, exterior Dutch doors invite air in low and a vented continuous ridge skylight and 9:12 roof slope facilitate the chimney and Bernoulli effects (see Heronwood Farm). Dormers, though primarily for aesthetic purposes on this barn, create a little more light and add some additional headroom for hay and bedding storage in the loft space.

Among Beechwood Stables' northern climate adaptations are a space for the muck wagon inside the barn. The space is recessed and isolated so the manure can remain separate and be driven directly out and hauled away, weather eventually permitting.

The barn is connected to the indoor 100-by-200-foot arena with wash and grooming stalls. The center aisle floor, along with flooring in the wash and grooming stalls, has radiant heat in an effort to make the environment more comfortable for humans. Again, horses thrive in an environment that is closer to nature (see Preface), so the stalls are not heated in this manner, and the stall area is continuously vented to the exterior, though controlled.

Instead of traditional roll-up doors on the arena, custom designed hangar-type doors were employed to create an overhang. If they need to be opened, they swing up to help protect the opening from the intrusion of driving rain or snow, also providing shade in summer from the hot sun. But perhaps paramount to that, in a horse arena, minimizing harsh shadows cast by window members, structural mullions, etc. is also a factor as they could cause a flight animal to jump or bolt in avoidance. Also, in lieu of sand in the arena, custom footing that does not require irrigation was used for ease of maintenance.

Possibly the most striking element of Beechwood Stables is its courtyard, accessed down a slight incline from the road so one is essentially below the road in what feels like a little gated community. A massive stone service building with open garage bays—

these portions hidden from anyone looking in from the street or entry road—provides definition and a sense of enclosure to the courtyard, with the indoor arena to the west, barn to the north, and outdoor arena flanked by woods to the east. Siting everything in this manner creates a quiet community isolating client and visitors from the road—a major east–west highway that parallels the turnpike—and its accruing noise and activity.

With appearance and color critical elements in barn design, and the barn visible from the road, a striking zinc-coated copper roof gilds the structure. Where initial discussions ran to nondescript asphalt shingle or else pure copper, because copper characteristically turns green over time the decision to use

zinc-coated copper satisfied the need for aesthetics, presence, and durability. From the road, the roof became the most visible portion of the courtyard structures due to its height relative to the height of the road. Rather than focus on a massive roof of asphalt shingle or a basic metal roof that would dominate one's first impression of the complex, the zinc-coated copper roof made for a more aesthetic statement.

Preparing for the elements and accommodating ADA issues as best we could while championing the animals, Beechwood Stables is another manifestation of all that is possible without sacrificing the health and safety of horses.

PEGASO FARM

Frank Lloyd Wright slept here

There's a right way and a wrong way to design a barn but there is no one way.

John Blackburn

Denizen of the Midwest and renowned for his iconic Prairie style of architecture, Frank Lloyd Wright built a multitude of residential and commercial properties in a manner defined by long, low, horizontal lines and forms. Though he built few barns, perhaps his most famous was Midway barn, aptly named for its location midway between Wright's home and the Hillside School at Taliesin.

When an industrialist client came to us with a challenge to build a 24-stall Prairie-style barn for dressage horses north of Chicago, naturally our own questions about optimal health for equines in a building without a steep roof slope for ventilation abounded. In fact, Wright's own Midway barn was not built in his signature Prairie style. Could we comply with the owner's mandate without compromising the health and safety of his horses? While the project would be exciting and surely fit the bill in terms of contextual design, it would be unlike any we'd done before as a low-slope roof does not facilitate the chimney or Bernoulli effects (see Heronwood Farm) in drawing air and humidity up and out. This, in turn, affects horses' sensitive respiratory systems as typical barn allergens and pathogens are less likely to be removed from the barn in a consistent, natural manner.

From the beginning, the client, a long-time Midwest resident, stated his design preference for Prairie-style architecture and an accruing barn as it was contextual to the area and his own lifestyle: he lived in an historic, Prairie-style residence. He was clear that the typical barn with tall, steep roof, cupolas, dormers, and an overuse of cross-bracing on barn doors was not for him. Though I was heartened by his desire to build something that was not typical in any sense of the word, I saw the challenge in marrying our signature barn approach, which is defined in part by steep roofs, with the Prairie-style low-sloped roof. In fact, though buoyed by his "outside the box" approach and passion for architecture, any thoughts of delight I had about his original concepts were soon mitigated by questions about his reasons for choosing our firm in the first place. Though we favor contextual design, our fundamental approach to barn design appeared to be the antithesis of the direction in which he wanted to go.

But in the course of his due diligence, the client had seen the range of our work and was confident we could meet his unique design goals.

As the site is at an intersection of a major north–south road and a secondary east–west road, we ensured privacy by creating a buffer zone of trees to conceal the farm. The entrance to the farm was selected off a secondary road with less traffic to provide both an element of safety from trailers pulling in and out, but also more privacy from those who may be curious to learn what is occurring behind the buffer of trees.

Upon entering the site, the service complex with vehicle/equipment storage, hay/bedding storage, and staff residences was located to the west and adjacent to existing wetlands but with required setbacks. This permitted better visual control of the entrance gate but also restricted service vehicles and other visitors to the entrance/front gate area. In turn this reinforced our concern for the health and safety of horses by confining them to the entrance area and permitted a lighter type of road construction to the barn site.

Barn and arena were located on the northwest corner at the end of the long entry drive, with the former becoming the focal point. Though the entry road bisects the site, it serves to isolate the service areas, storm water retention ponds, wetlands to the west of the driveway, and paddocks to the east. Subsequently horses, people, and vehicles are all isolated but join at precisely the point where they need to.

With the property located on 24 acres just a few miles from Lake Michigan, issues of snow, ice, and austere winter winds both from the lake to the East and also from the Northwest would also drive our design which included the barn, indoor and outdoor arenas, service and storage buildings, and owner and staff residences. Though we ended up siting the barn perpendicular to the prevailing summer breeze, as we most always do and in this case to mitigate the Midwest's hot, humid summers, we decided that based on the region's omnipresent winds we could actually forego a steep roof pitch without compromising the natural ventilation germane to our designs.

Conversely, to offset the region's extreme winter climate, incorporating architectural devices such as placing the indoor arena on the backside of the barn to block that season's excess cold northwest winds served the property well. Seen from the other side or from the entrance drive as the barn is approached, the barn breaks up the massive scale of the 22,000-square-foot arena.

To collect natural light and establish ventilation, a continuous ridge skylight was used down the barn's center aisle, though this one was relatively flat to maintain the design by paralleling the roof. While the roof does have some slope—1.5:12 over the stall areas and 2:12 over the center aisle, as opposed to our typical 7:12 or 8:12—it basically floats over the barn.

The roof is also vented under the eaves and the top of the wall on one side is equipped with louvers, and above-stall transoms also channel natural light and open for air. In this regard, though not creating the exact desired chimney and Bernoulli effects (see Heronwood Farm), ventilation was created by focusing the region's natural winds at a level above the horse. Requisite Dutch doors were also used to bring air in low in warmer weather, as in the majority of our barns, but in the dead of winter these Midwestern horses can be kept in their stalls out of any drafts, Dutch doors closed, and the barn can still ventilate.

Additionally, the flat roof was conceived to slope to the rear, or northwest side, so snow would slide off to that side of the barn which is relatively inaccessible. Entrances at the ends and in front of the barn are

subsequently protected from snow piling up outside of them, creating a smoother transition for owner, staff, and horses.

Extremely flat and encumbered with wetlands typically found in Illinois, the site's soil retains a lot of water and generally stays soggy. Accordingly, appropriate drainage could become a problem for the animals who would be using the paddocks and outdoor arena. A decision was made to create drain swells, which drained the paddocks, elevated the buildings and gave the land a little more definition and interest. Similar to some of the site challenges we encounter in designing other barns (Lucky Jack Farm among our most striking examples), this is another instance of proverbially turning lemons into lemonade. The barn was actually elevated 2 feet to provide positive drainage away from it. In this respect we got to raise the barn floor

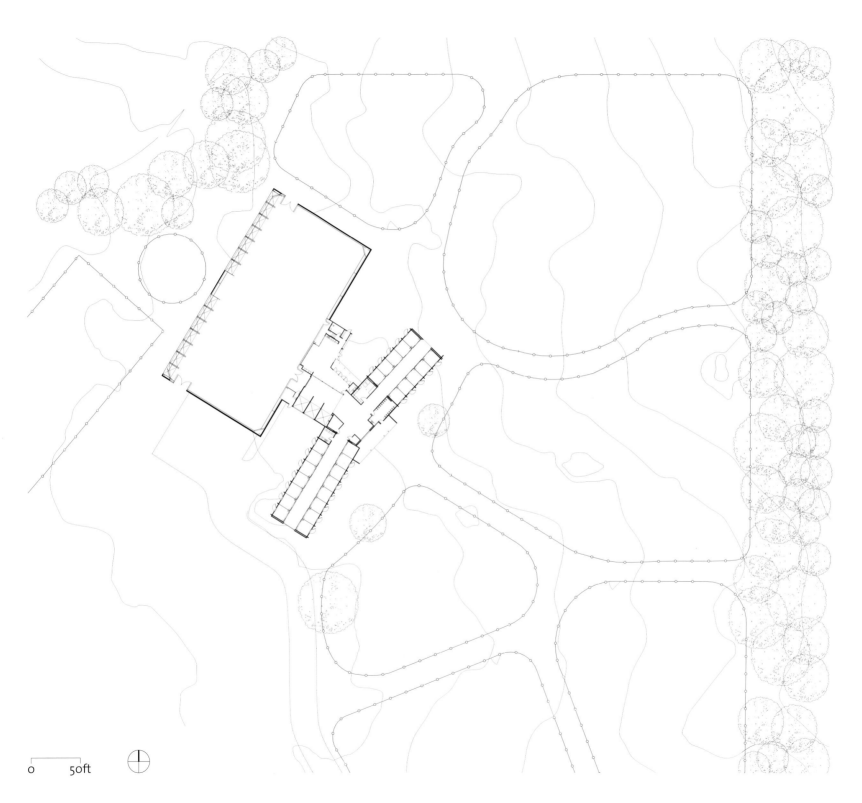

0   50ft

higher than the arena floor, the latter of which was simultaneously pushed down about two feet— so the 4-foot discrepancy visually reduces the arena's scale.

While the barn is symmetrical to a large extent, a middle section with raised roof for a little more definition—and clearly to designate the entrance for visitors—is marked by a fire separation wall that isolates the stalls from the human and service areas. Conceived to house a tack room, laundry room, and basic feed storage, a heated floor with interlocking rubber brick makes the mid section's environment comfortable for staff in the wintertime. The center portion leads to the indoor arena ramp. Several wash and grooming stalls and holding stalls that can be used for a farrier or veterinarian flank the ramp. In fact, the farrier or vet can drive down a small lane between the barn and arena and pull directly up to this cross-connecting link or ramp to work in a partially heated indoor space. The exterior space between the barn and arena provides an area protected from

winter winds, however, permitting the farrier or vet to work outdoors by their truck most of the year if they need to.

An observation area for the arena features a kitchen, fireplace, and living room/office, with the advantage of seeing over into the connecting link or ramp to the arena. In kinder weather, an outdoor terrace area provides incentive for entertaining or just relaxing.

In terms of durability and aesthetics, both painted Hardiplank siding and Western red cedar siding were used for the exterior. Typically, Dutch doors are used to give rhythm to a building—to break it up, but in the case of Prairie-style architecture, the objective was to accentuate its horizontality without breaking it up. Accordingly, the inside of the Dutch doors were lined with the same Western red cedar, so that when flush against the building instead of standing out they blend in with the exterior to maintain its elongated look and form. Because the client developed and

manufactured floor mats for cars, he was aware of the product's tendency to off-gas harmful chemicals. When he decided to expand into producing equine interlocking rubber brick and mats for stalls, using the Pegaso Farm barn as a prototype, he created a product that is better engineered and thereby healthier both for animals and the humans who work around them. What's more, the new mats are much lighter than traditional stall mats, providing an easier task for the workers who have to clean and haul them in and out of stalls.

For Pegaso Farm, balancing the client's desires for an atypical Prairie-style barn in a climate of extreme weather conditions without sacrificing the health and safety of horses was a challenge, but one that we believe we met considerably well. In doing so, we included three essential elements for any successful equestrian project: a balance of the goals of owner, the demands of the site, and the needs of the horse—without sacrificing any of these needs to design.

ALL'S WELL FARM
hunt country heaven

*The health of the horse can be
affected by every aspect of the farm
from the layout of the roads and
paddocks down to the selection and
placement of the buckets in the stall.*

John Blackburn

In creating a horse farm for two New England ex-pats and their young daughter in Northern Virginia's idyllic hunt country, one of the objectives was to incorporate elements of both regions into the design.

Located on 88 acres amid gently rolling hills and long, pristine country roads, All's Well Farm was born on a largely empty parcel of land. Interestingly, things came full circle when Keith LeBlanc Landscape Architecture out of Boston connected us with the client. I had worked with LeBlanc in the early 1980s on Heronwood Farm—our very first farm— when he was part of Morgan Wheelock's firm. For All's Well Farm, LeBlanc focused on the residence and gardens and our work was on siting and barn design.

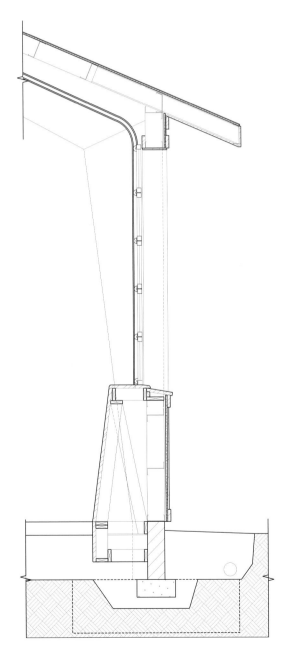

Except for an older residence whose renovation fell largely under the baton of a Boston-area interior design firm, Cebula Design, with which the client had previously worked, the site was a clean canvas for our work. Designed for a dressage-focused owner, the 8-stall barn was to include two larger foaling stalls, an approximately 65-by-200-foot indoor/outdoor arena plus a separate open arena, observation room with entertaining capabilities, tack room, and office with guest space above the tack room.

Exterior Dutch doors and a continuous vented ridge skylight, along with vented eaves and a 10:12 roof slope, would allow the barn to breathe as all of ours do by pulling air in low and venting it out high.

Sited perpendicular to the prevailing southwest summer breeze, the barn was also constructed parallel to the entry road. In this respect when driving onto the property the arena is purposely not visible, dropping several feet down the hill behind the barn and perpendicular to it. This helps conceal the arena due to its length. In fact, this arrangement works perfectly for a dressage arena where the observation area is typically located along its narrow end—the first judge's position in competition. To ensure additional privacy the barn itself isn't even visible from the main road, with passersby aware only of a slight rise and fall of the land.

In meeting the client's desire to meld something of the wife's deep New England roots with Virginia horse country vernacular, the connecting link between barn and arena is clad in wood cedar shingles. The rest of the barn and arena are designed with horizontal Hardiplank siding. The decision to use both styles worked well aesthetically as using one or the other all the way through would have resulted in a monotonous exterior.

In the arena, control-operated roll-up doors facilitate the indoor/outdoor space easily transitioning from winter to summer, framing the rich, pastoral Virginia countryside view in

milder months. A 5-foot rail allows the rider to see out but keeps the horse's proverbial nose to the grindstone. At All's Well Farm, there is also an arena skylight for maximum light during colder seasons when the structure doors are closed up, though doors are glass to court as much year round natural light as possible.

Working with Cebula Design who selected the interior finishes, the double-height observation room was clad in reclaimed river-dredged Yellow Pine with Douglas fir posts. The roof was designed to utilize solar panels for self-sufficient energy and to collect rainwater for recycling when the client is ready for additional installation.

Large dormers appear at the cross-aisle and the connecting link, the latter providing a view into the loft. Another dormer channels light into the observation area.

Though the brunt of the riding was to fall to his wife and daughter, the client had many interests and was earnestly learning to ride. To help cultivate and further develop his interest in astronomy, we were asked to build an observatory on the property for a highly sophisticated telescope that had been presented as a retirement gift. Our mandate was for a specially designed foundation to help eliminate vibrations. Located out in the country, the telescope and its housing provided an unobstructed view of the night sky free of light pollution.

The barn at All's Well Farm is the ideal structure for a private owner and her young daughter who love to ride, and for a husband who is a determined student. It evokes elements of their former New England environs and their adopted Virginia home.

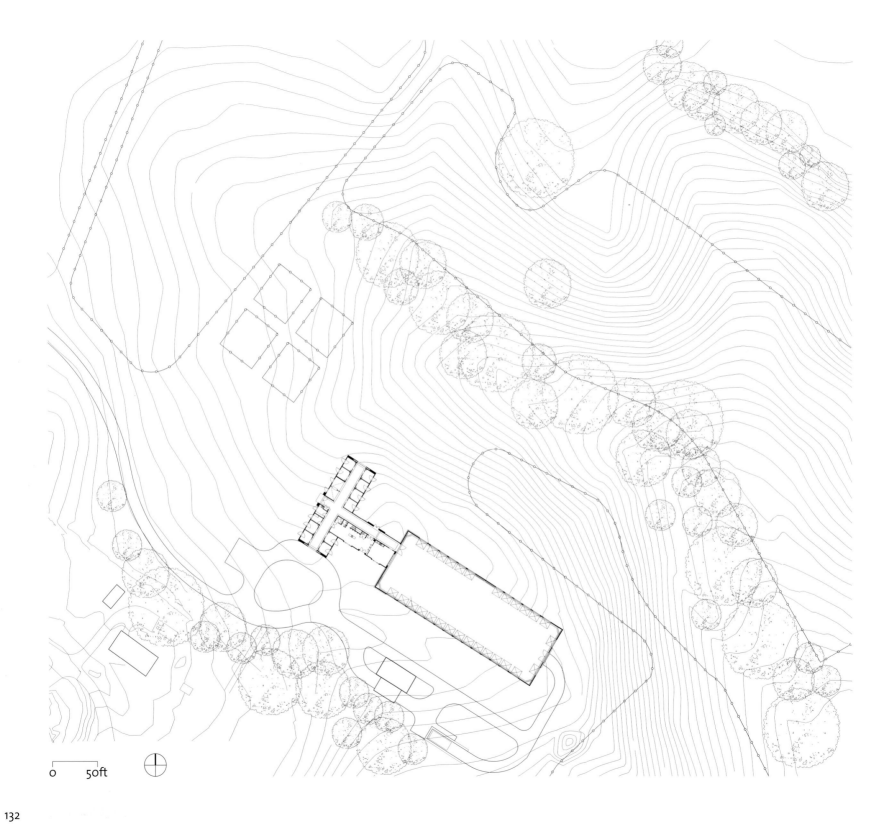

0   50ft

PRIVATE RANCH, MONTANA
trail blazing and day stretching

The equine architect must "listen" to the site the same way an equestrian listens to his horse. Much like a horse with his individual demands and personality, a site contains its own demands and personality. You must find and work with them for the project to be successful.

John Blackburn

For a California-based client with wrangling dreams, home on the range—a Montana ranch for at least a few months out of the year—became a bracing reality for him and his growing family.

Sited on 88,000 acres along the Lewis and Clark Trail, the rocky, agrestic terrain was primed to indulge a businessman's penchant for roping and riding, along with the challenge of raising cattle. Because of its expanse it would also facilitate an airstrip for his plane, and clearly support his desire to impart the values of hard work and good horsemanship to his young children.

Commissioned to plan a portion of the ranch, the 6,000-square-foot, 8-stall main barn we designed would need to accommodate Quarter horses and tack for Western-style riding, and

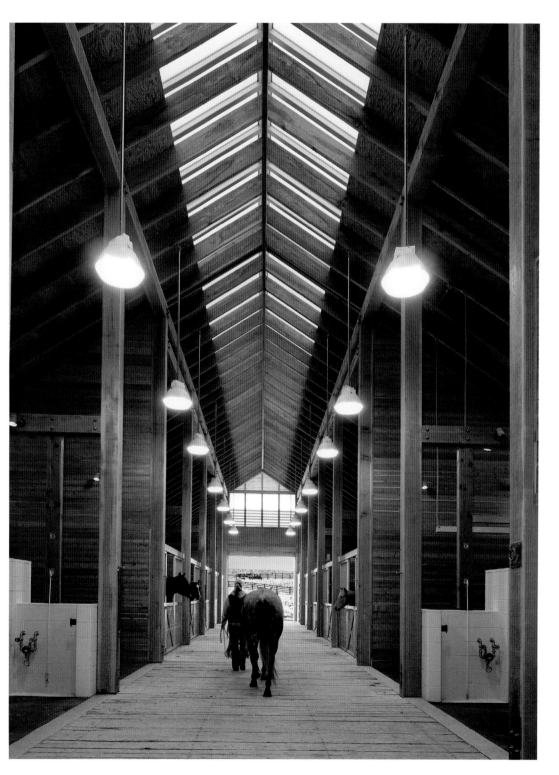

more preened English Hunter Jumper horses and their accoutrements—the latter for his wife. Interestingly, the client also opted for both family and guest tack rooms, something we rarely do, which required a longer building. A planned indoor arena was later sacrificed to various issues including a necessary land change, but the 4,500-square-foot outdoor arena—rimmed by recycled oil pipes—would more than fit the bill for an active family, ranch hands, and visitors.

With the ranch residence designed by architecture, planning, and interior design firm Bohlin Cywinsky Jackson, and essentially under construction when we became involved, we decided to reiterate some of the heavy timber, bolt connections, metal roof, wood siding, massive cedar log columns, and cedar interiors mandated for the home in the barn, though the barn's budget was considerably less.

Inside the barn, the client's wife—certainly adventurous from an architectural standpoint—presented a compelling argument for a galvanized stall system. Desiring that the framing, bars, doors and everything else that is metal, which are typically powder-coated steel, be executed in galvanized steel,

it would be the first time we had ever done things this way. But her agenda to control rust and deterioration in the often punishing Montana climate was a valid one. While our initial thinking was that the finished product could be industrial-looking and cumbersome instead of exhibiting a more refined aesthetic emblematic of our barns, the contrast of the warm wood and mottled look of the galvanized steel produced a spectacular result.

For this barn, in addition to our recommended steep roof slope of 8:12 which, with elements like exterior Dutch doors seen in most of our barns, helps facilitate optimal ventilation in

creating the chimney and Bernoulli effects (see Heronwood Farm), our objective is always to honor the surroundings in terms of contextual design. In short, we wanted to do something that reflected the Western vernacular and profound sense of history evident around every bend on this ranch. To that end, we discovered a characteristic old barn on the property, amidst splintered headstones marking the final resting places of settlers killed by Indians, an ax incident, and even a 19th-century murder-suicide. The roof slope of this barn was 8:12, extending out and down to 4:12, something I immediately recognized as the right contextual shape for our new barn.

What we did differently, however, was to modernize the design by raising a section to create a vent and in which to locate the skylight. We took this even further by extending the skylight beyond the exterior wall so that it cantilevers out with the hay hoods (a typical detail over a hayloft, though

storage is elsewhere which we recommend for respiratory health and fire safety reasons), with a loft space and balcony. This is a great observation point from which to peruse the outdoor arena, just 20 yards away, with guests and a cool (or warm!) drink and a view down aisle of the barn. The polycarbonate material used for this and most of our skylights was also utilized to create translucent wall panels for the Montana barn to channel light inside at every opportunity. As the region is defined by long, cold winters and short, bleak days, stretching the day as we did was a significant objective.

Though we typically site a barn perpendicular to the prevailing summer breeze for preferred ventilation purposes, as seen in previous chapters, the property's contouring mandated that we locate this one in a way that also worked with the slope of the terrain—ultimately a northwest/southeast orientation—though we still achieved the desired result. Because the terrain was generally elevated with few

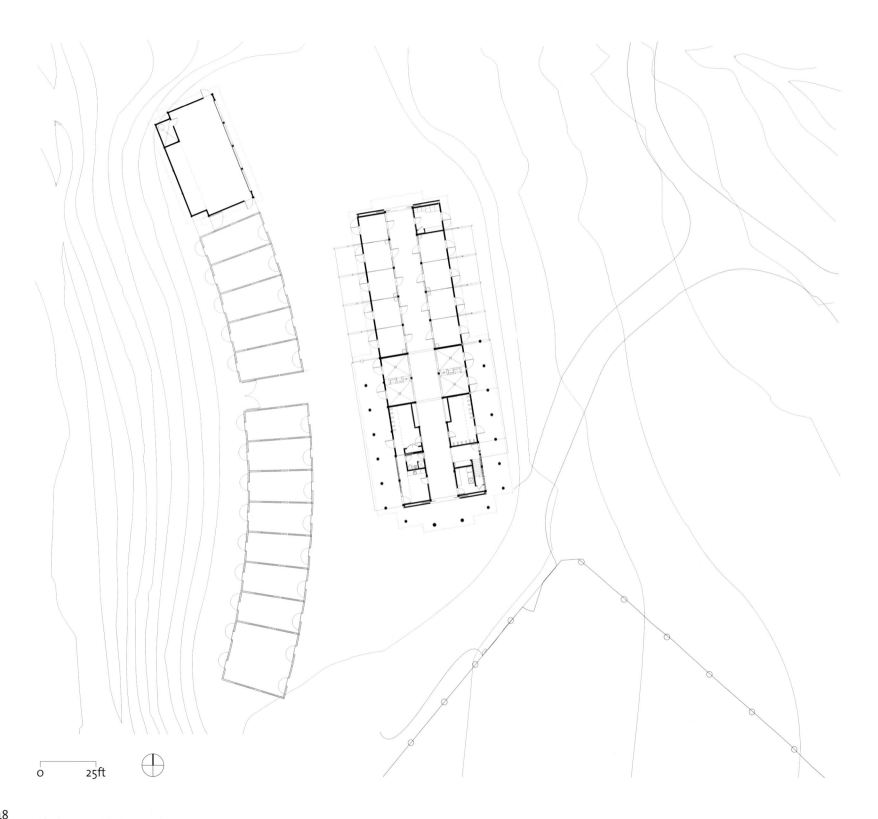

0   25ft

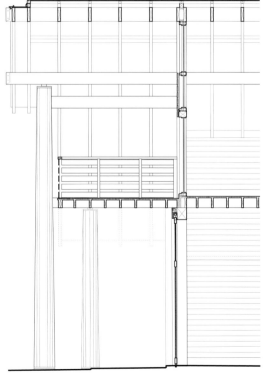

trees and other elements to block the natural winds, it became a fairly simple matter to take advantage of natural ventilation from virtually any direction.

A succession of covered exterior holding corrals were built here in Montana. In this regard, horses turned out to pasture can later be herded into smaller paddocks and then to these covered corrals, until they are ultimately used in the ranch's cattle operation or perhaps directed to roping activities in the arena or just groomed. Also outside, deep overhangs create two covered areas for washing and grooming in warmer weather, along with four indoor wash stalls for other months. According to local weather pundits, Montana temperature fluctuations can range from minus 30 degrees Fahrenheit one day to 30 above the next, and rise to 60 degrees the following week.

Flooring was originally conceived as popcorn asphalt but as the barn was already under construction, it was changed at the request of the owner to cottonwood—indigenous to the region and fittingly found in many Louis L'Amour novels. We excavated down several feet, as far as we could go without exposing foundations already in place, added gravel and drains and created airspace so the space would "breathe," reducing the risk of odor build-up and so the flooring wouldn't rot. The eight 14-by-14-foot stalls have rubber mats on stone dust.

Overall, the Montana ranch is clean and contemporary but with an historic connection to its rich western roots. Context and roots are an objective for all of our designs. This was one of our first Western-style riding-focused barns and set a materials and aesthetic precedent for others to come.

GREAT ROAD FARM
an abled life

A barn does not have to cost you an

arm and a leg, but neither should a

poor barn design cost you your horse.

John Blackburn

One of the more enjoyable parts of my work in designing a horse farm, beyond the pleasure of having it built and come to life, is seeing the excitement expressed in the face of a satisfied client. This satisfaction is often demonstrated and perpetuated in the manner in which they use the barn and farm, and that's certainly the case with Great Road Farm.

As Connecticut transplants to Montgomery Township on the outskirts of Princeton, New Jersey, the clients—he, a former franchise owner with 37 restaurants in his saddle bag and she, a licensed social worker—desired a different kind of life for themselves and their four sons. Jettisoning the frenetic franchise world, the husband favored farming and food.

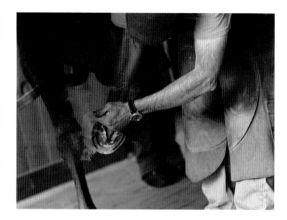

He went to culinary school and worked for a top New York restaurant before opening his own farm-to-table eatery in Princeton near Great Road Farm. The wife sought to parlay her expertise in social work into a therapeutic riding facility on their new farm. Accordingly, our imperative was to construct a 12-stall barn for Hunter Jumpers and indoor and outdoor riding arenas. The first of the two arenas would do double duty for family and friends as well as accommodate disabled students.

Created in a straightforward style for owners who enjoy traditional New England architecture, and who coveted elements like a cupola over the cross aisle, the barn makes a clean, uncomplicated statement.

Though we typically site our barns perpendicular to the prevailing summer breeze in order to maximize ventilation without the use of cumbersome fans in doorways that blow particles, allergens, and pathogens into the horses' sensitive respiratory systems (see Heronwood Farm), in this case we chose to modify the slope of the land to orient the barn. Utilizing the natural breezes that blow across surrounding fields was the goal. Had we sited it directly with the slope in a simpler, cost-saving measure, the barn would have been positioned 90 degrees in a different direction, succumbing to the region's summer heat and humidity. In all locations, though there may be a prevailing wind pattern, that pattern may be altered by ground conditions such as terrain

and vegetation. At Great Road Farm, while we were hindered by the slope, the large forested area to the south caused wind patterns to shift more from the west. Siting the barn as we did allowed us to exploit that natural summer wind pattern.

As another preventative measure, we decided to site the barn perpendicular to the property's parallel contours so the barn is on a north/south orientation to capture the aforementioned breeze. Typically the barn is built parallel to the contours, but doing so in this case would have courted winter's harsh north winds as they whipped across the open field, creating a truly miserable situation for man and beast.

Using exterior Dutch doors and our standard 8:12 roof slope and ventilated skylight to create the desired chimney and Bernoulli effects (see Heronwood Farm), in this barn we also used louvered, triangular dormers for architectural interest and style and some additional ventilation.

On the interior, which is pine with Douglas fir columns, the cross aisle is off-center which aids in the efficiency of operation for a 12-stall barn. Pocket doors can isolate the barn's center portion—with its service areas—from the stall area. In this regard, because horses thrive in an environment that is as close to nature as possible, and the service areas may be more temperature-controlled, this creates optimal living conditions for the animals. Custom-designed cubby holes along one side of the cross-aisle facilitate easy storage of riders' and instructors' personal effects. The barn floor is actual brick, something more cost-effective than the interlocking rubber brick we use in many of our buildings. That said, many clients also relish the clippity-clop sound of their horses' hoofs on a more natural surface such as brick anyway. The exterior is Hardiplank board-and-batten.

Though not yet executed, the barn at Great Road Farm was designed to have a connecting link with roof for coverage en route from the building's end to the indoor therapeutic riding arena, which has large sliding windows on all sides and a ridge skylight, with the roof framed in open web wood trusses. The connecting link concept impacted the farm's layout as the arena was sited at the north end and set up to isolate the public from the horses, yet allow the latter to go from barn to arena without going outside. The arena was also located so that it was partially concealed by the forested area to the south,

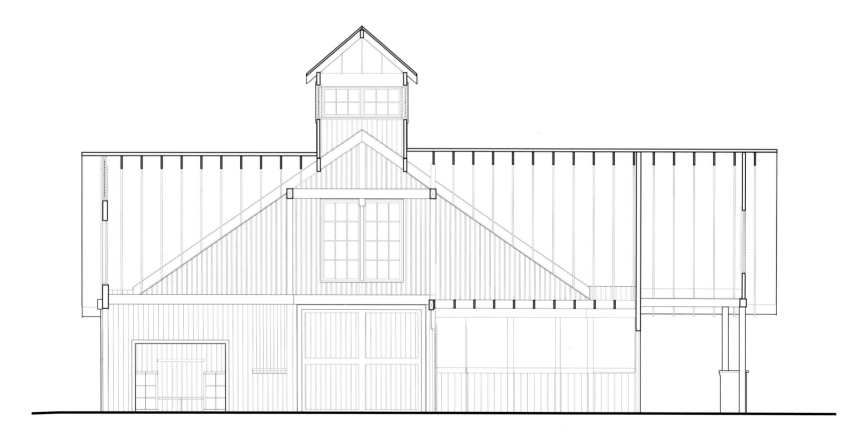

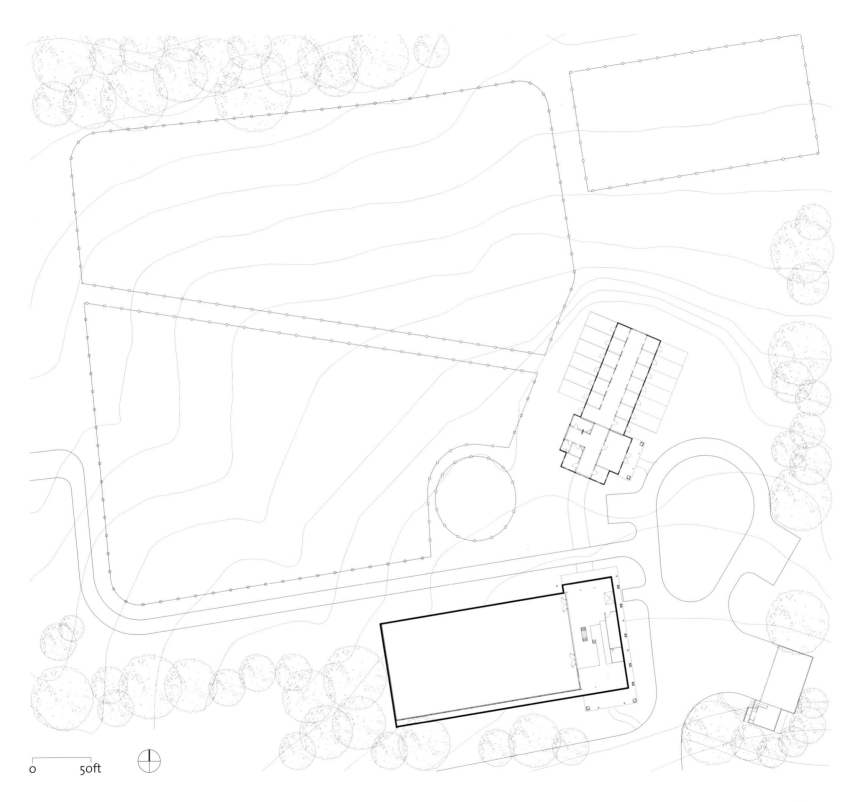

0   50ft

allowing us to push it into the natural slope of the hill. This provided for a reduction in scale relative to the barn, something we always try to achieve so as not to have the larger, plainer, box-like arena dominating the complex.

Additionally, public access to the arena and barn complex is through the forested area, providing for entry from natural grade onto a raised viewing platform if desired. In this respect, accompanying family, caregivers, and friends of the riding students have a strong visual connection to both the arena and the barn complex. The arena has full accessibility for the physically impaired, based on siting it using the natural terrain.

While the barn was created without the grandeur of some of our other equine projects, it is as functional, healthy, and safe as any. It also contains custom features, such as a spacious office/lounge combination and covered entrance porch on the east side. Physically challenged individuals can either be transported from car into the barn if that is their program, or straight to the arena without having to traverse the barn.

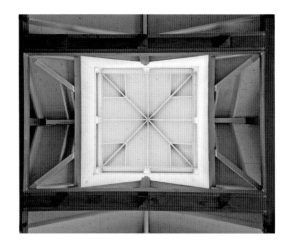

GLENWOOD FARM
southern charm and cordiality

There is no one ultimate (perfect)

barn except the one that works

for you.

John Blackburn

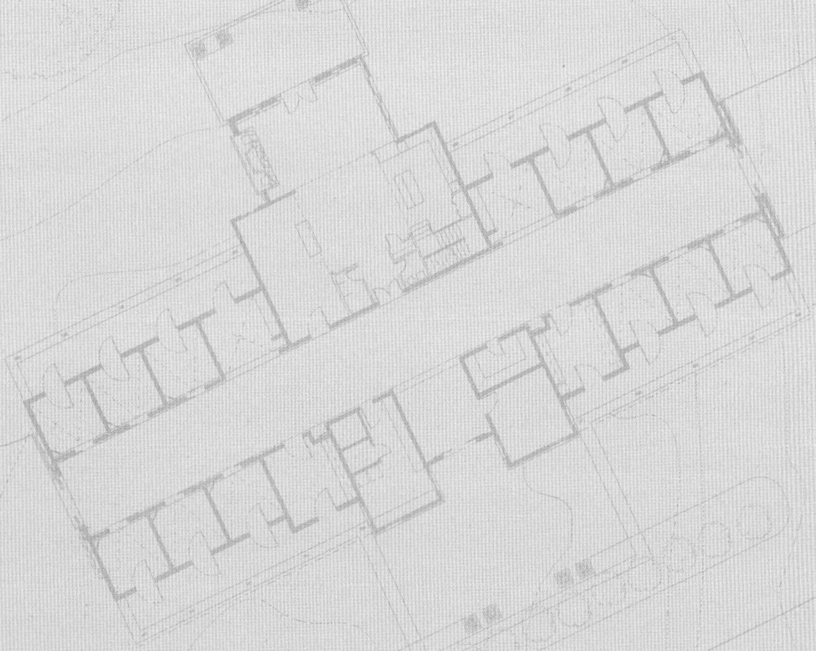

For the hard-charging head of a transportation firm specializing in the design of highways, bridges, and airports, a pastoral place to recharge and regroup was the program for a Ridgeway, South Carolina barn design.

With the 233-acre parcel defined by two pleasing ponds and a lot of open space, and while the client was not a horseman in the traditional sense, he took a gentleman farmer approach in his desire to own horses and provide them with a custom environment. Friends of his rode and would be invited to board their horses. In this case, as with many of our clients, the barn and arena had to be both functional and inviting—fit for sheltering Hunter Jumpers as well as entertaining equestrian guests and others. What's more, a requisite bedroom loft and lower living space, replete with large kitchen and dining room, had to provide accommodations for him from time to time while a residence was constructed amidst the towering pines across one of the ponds— one that would look back at the barn.

When we first arrived at the site, an existing dirt entrance road lined with pine trees extended into the property about 300 yards. A clearing was next (with an old, abandoned trailer that had to be removed) atop a knoll with a panoramic view of a pond to the north and open fields—former cow pastures—to the left and right. There was also a magnificent stand of tall pines across the larger pond directly in front, all of which left no doubt this was the perfect location for the barn. Positioning it on top of a natural rise in the land would optimize vistas and summer breezes.

Inasmuch as this was South Carolina with its characteristic hot and humid climate for most of the year, siting the barn to capture prevailing summer wind patterns for the horses to thrive was at the top of the program. As mentioned in previous chapters, we frequently rely on airport wind data when available to determine wind patterns and amount of wind generated at other times of the year, which, particularly in northern climes, can be the difference between a comfortable barn and a great deal of misery for horse, rider, and staff in winter.

Though contours of the land and other factors sometimes mitigate an exact siting, as they did here, we came close enough with a north/south orientation. Exterior Dutch doors facilitate the desired chimney and Bernoulli effects (see Heronwood Farm) so that air continuously circulates up and out through an extruded

aluminum frame skylight. The skylight is raised by a foot to increase the amount of ventilation and allow for operable louvers to control the airflow—and separate it from the standing seam metal roof with its 9:12 roof slope.

Inspired by what he knew of another project of ours, the client flew his plane to Texas Hill Country to investigate Oakhaven Farm, where the barn's singular stonework and heavy Douglas fir timber help define it, as does its metal roof. Though adapted for the region and style, these elements are echoed on Glenwood's exterior and in fact the same builder, Jack Hart of Advance Construction was retained.

As with Oakhaven and its 16-stall barn, Glenwood's 12-stall barn was constructed of masonry block concrete for fireproofing reasons, and to guard against the Southeast's mildew and "resident" infestation matters, clad in certain areas with the stonework and also Hardiplank.

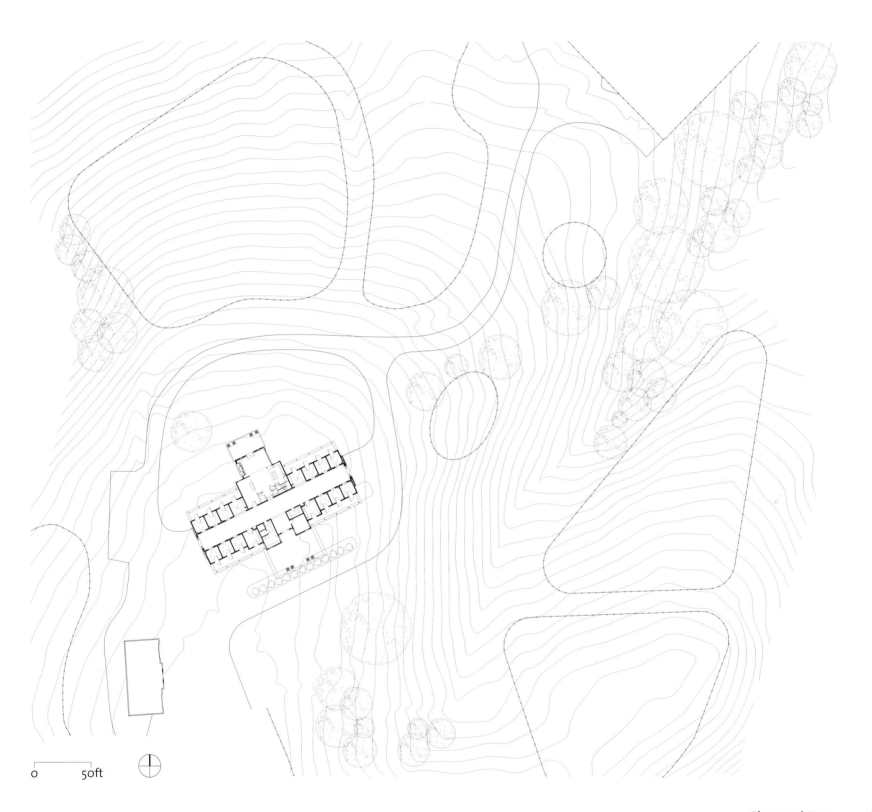

0   50ft

To maximize the sense of arrival on this beautiful property, we terminated the entry in a circular drive in front of the cross-aisle of the barn, flanked on the left by a service storage building and on the right by a small staff residence creating an informal courtyard. A heavy timber porte-cochere was functional in shielding horse and rider from the intense sun at that juncture, or from the rain in loading and unloading of trailers, and also defined the front entrance as one approached along the entry drive. Often one enters a barn through the barn aisle door at the end, but because of the strong axis created by the entry drive, here one is directed to the middle. Additionally, because the barn would be used for boarding, safety is ensured by encouraging visitors unfamiliar with the structure to enter through a "controlled" entry point, much like a front door, as opposed to wandering directly into the main aisle.

Aesthetically, visitors entering in this way are treated to a dramatic pond view as well as the barn's desirable great room, which is a combination of a cathedral-ceilinged full kitchen and lounge, dining room, living room with stone fireplace and flat screen TV, and showcase-style (not just utilitarian) tack room.

Along with an outside terrace for everyone's use, the client wanted to be sure his guests were part of his gracious lifestyle. Oak wainscoting along the aisle and in the horse stalls and wrought iron chandeliers and accent candle-style lighting augment the fine finishes. The covered terrace with lounge at the barn's north side overlooks one of the ponds, and the aforementioned heavy timber porte-cochere punctuates the barn's south side. Along the barn's exterior, an overhang on the outside

of the stalls provides shade for the animals as they look out through yoke gates and serves to keep the barn itself cooler.

Outdoors, a 100-by-200-foot steel frame arena with louvered skylight is open on the sides but covered, again protecting equines and riders from the relentless South Carolina sun.

What distinguishes Glenwood Farm from some of our other properties is the nature of its high-quality tack room, extensive kitchen, and lounge—which make it a lot more like home for both horses and humans. A successful design must respond to the demands of the site, and Glenwood Farm is a fine example of achieving this in tandem with meeting the owner's needs as well as those of the horses.

PRIVATE STABLE, CALIFORNIA
the gilding of the green (barn)

The design of the horse farm is

contained within the site. Our

challenge as designers is to find it

and give it life.

John Blackburn

Defined by lush trees, striking scenery, hilly terrain, distant mountains, extensive trail systems, and a dry, moderate climate, an IT executive, his wife, and three daughters were drawn to an historic California horse community. Purchasing a 10-acre property, the goal was a residence and horse farm for the family's cadre of Hunter Jumpers.

Typical of a number of horse communities throughout the country that seek to control their equine population and aesthetic, including road space and building size, the area's approval board restrictions were almost innumerable. The time involved in conceptualizing, presenting, revising, presenting again and maybe going through

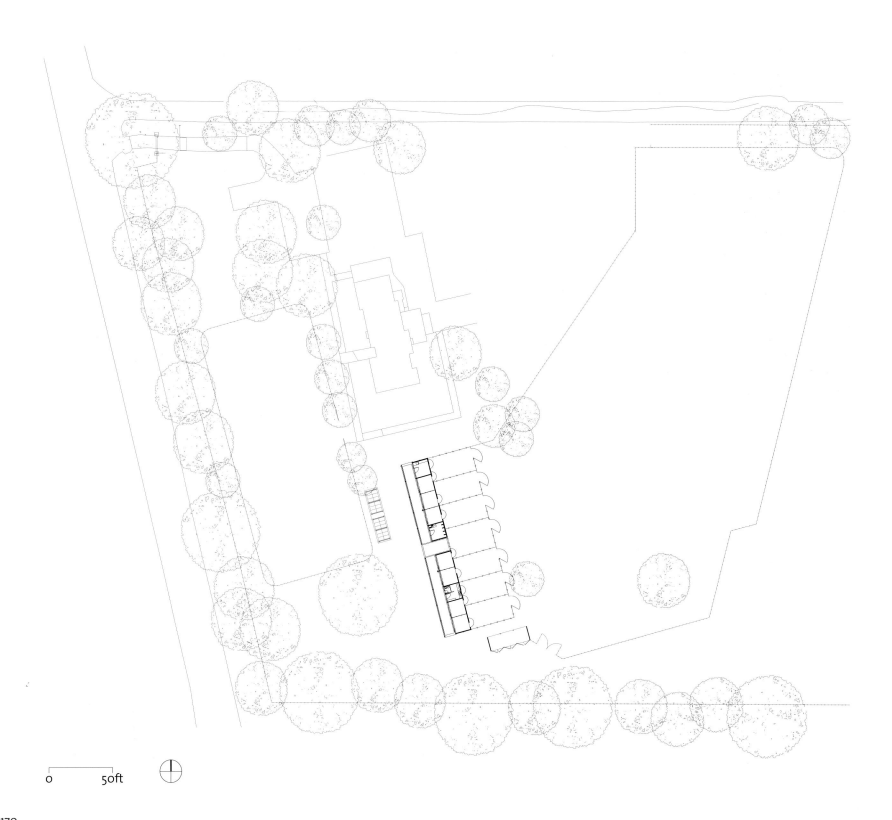

0   50ft

the same process three, four, and five times with the review board had proved daunting for many. In fact, in the past, I'd had two clients in the area simply give up.

In this case and possibly attributed to the demands of his profession, the client was highly disciplined, paid meticulous attention to detail, and maybe paramount to that was extremely persistent. What's more, the family had been boarding no fewer than eight horses elsewhere in this pricey community and was anxious to call the proverbial troops home.

Desiring a 7-stall barn (one of the horses was rehomed), the client also wished to demolish an existing house on the property and build a new one. Working with local firm Square Three Design Studios LLC, chosen by the owner for the residence, we were commissioned

to develop a master plan for the equestrian portion of the property. This included a barn that both addressed the health and safety of horses and reflected the home's contemporary design, most prominently a barrel vaulted roof. An outdoor arena was also on the agenda.

As my firm had formerly developed plans for a group of four distinct regionally-sensitive and predesigned *Blackburn Green Barns*™, characterized in part by their sustainable, local materials and economic appeal, the client decided he liked one in particular: *The Hickory*. Created in a shed row-style for warmer climates (for an example of shed row-style see Ketchen Place Farm), with features that included a single-loaded aisle and open concept design, he asked us to adapt and customize it so that it maintained its function

but again echoed some of the residence's most prominent design features, mainly the barrel vault roof.

Using *The Hickory* as a foundation, customizing it involved creating more of a finished design. The original plan had exposed rafters, for example, and the client chose to laminate them under the smooth, curved, barrel vault roof for a more refined aesthetic.

As with Ketchen Place Farm, *The Hickory* has no skylight though does have ample clerestory windows and vents for natural light and considerable ventilation. Louvers at each end of the barn provide additional high wall vents and Dutch doors on stall exteriors help facilitate low venting. Because of the curved roof, wind blows across it similar to

the way air would go up and over the wing of a plane, helping to maintain healthy conditions in the interior.

The property presented a design challenge in itself. Of the 10 acres, approximately the back 1/5 to 1/3 was wetlands: tall grasses and small scrubs. The land also presented itself in a straight slope at a high point down from the main road, all the way to a low point by the wetlands, and near the front of the property were a lot of live oaks, walnut trees, and others that were in the way—

some of substantial size—and a limited number had to be removed. Because of the wetlands, we could not position the arena in back. The middle third of the property was open—perfect for paddocks.

While the inclination would be to site the barn and arena toward the front, uphill, where the slope is higher and drains away, one also needs to exercise vigilance where accruing service roads and outdoor wash stalls can impact the trees. Fortunately *The Hickory* is designed as

a straight line, which works well with the slope of the land, but the challenge lay in the town's strenuous approval process as it would be highly visible from the road. Again and largely attributed to the client's meticulous attention to detail and great persistence, the design was ultimately approved. In fact in a subsequent year, my firm received a call from a review board member who wished to explore building one of our barns on her own property.

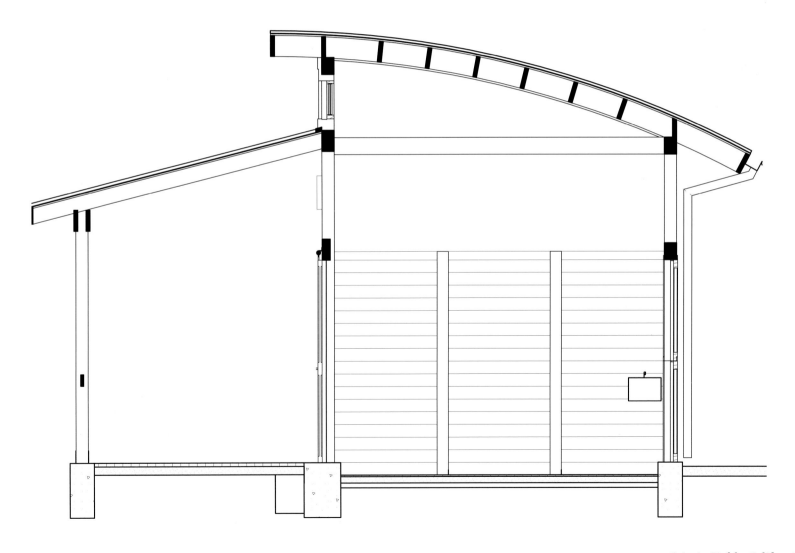

Also high on the client's agenda was that each horse had access from an indoor stall to an outdoor one, or turnout, the latter of which is several times the size of the former, extending back about 24 feet. In this respect horses could move in and out at will, availing themselves of the fresh air or maneuvering out of the hot sun or any inclement weather. The outdoor stalls or turnouts were also to connect to the main paddocks, and access to such could be individually controlled by staff.

On the exterior, a metal roof and Douglas fir siding complete the look of the refined *Hickory* barn. The client also opted for an efficient *O2 Compost* system for manure, something we usually recommend for natural decomposition. The system is onsite and manure does not have to be trucked elsewhere, in deference to environmental concerns.

The 100-by-235-foot arena is located in front between the barn and road, and along the road is an existing woodside trail where horses travel all the time. By placing the stalls at the back, as we ultimately did, the finer part of the barn faces out to create a pleasing aesthetic. Also, by creating a barn that is open to sunlight and wind currents, no artificial lights are needed anywhere during the day, even in the tack room, which minimizes its carbon footprint and incidences of barn fires attributed to overburdened electrical systems.

Because of the site restraints and stringent approval process, designing and executing this horse farm took us longer than any other we've done of its size—approximately the same amount of time it would take to create some of our larger projects that comprised hundreds of acres. But what is perhaps most compelling about this private stable is that it is fundamentally a green barn, augmented and contemporized with unusual features such as the barrel vault roof, which makes it a truly custom barn.

AFTERWORD

Years ago, as my children began to grow, find themselves, and focus on their own interests, I told them not to look for a specific job but rather to find their passion. The rest will come. Though hard work and a little luck are intrinsic to the end result, a powerful connection to what one does in this world can mean the difference between a life well spent and one that simply passes by.

Growing up, I'd learned that I liked construction and working with my hands. Dinner table discussions about conserving fuel and recycling materials in WWII, my parents' hard work and struggle in running a business, and the largely rural environment in which I was raised helped develop my values and hone my world view.

When I ultimately found architecture as a natural expression of what meant the most to me, one might say the die was cast and in time I was designing structures that sheltered and supported people and their passion, which happened to be horses, as well as reflecting and preserving aspects of the regions in which they were built both contextually and through their use of materials.

Designs for the horse farms and stables in this book have evolved from Heronwood—our first venture—to the storied, behemoth Thoroughbred breeding facility Sagamore Farm, to California's Devine Ranch with its meandering code and environmental restrictions, to iterations such as the Midwest's Pegaso Farm, built around the principles of Frank Lloyd Wright's Prairie style architecture.

In all cases the needs of the owner and parameters of the site and environment provided a backdrop for our primary concern: the health and safety of horses. As an architect, designing barns that achieve these goals through a confluence of science and design is a passion well realized. And I'm just getting started.

ACKNOWLEDGEMENTS

I wish to personally thank the following people for their inspiration and contribution in creating this book:

Morgan Wheelock for his inspiration and mentoring of my former partner and me in the theories of designing for the health and safety for horses, and introducing us to Robert H. Smith, our first equestrian client.

Robert H. Smith for trusting in two young architects to design Heronwood Farm, his new thoroughbred breeding farm and our first equestrian project.

Vicky Moon whose knowledge of "who's who, who was who, and what counts" in the equine community is incomparable, and who has been invaluable in introducing me to that community.

Carolyn Willekes, Ph.D., whose meticulous research and multilingual skills resulted in the acquisition of key information on the detailed history of stabling—so much that I've reserved some for the next book!

My staff:

Daniel Blair, Matt Himler, Ian Kelly, and **Cesar Lujan** for their assistance in pulling together all the drawings included in an undertaking of this proportion. I owe a special debt of gratitude to Cesar Lujan for his expert photographic work for many of the projects and for managing the process of creating, assembling, and editing all the artwork and photographs included in this book.

PROJECT TEAMS

Introduction
Photographers:
Cesar Lujan: Pages 12–13
David Hartig: Page 13 top
Tre Dunham: Page 13 bottom
Kenneth M. Wyner: Pages 14–15

Heronwood Farm
Landscape Architect: Morgan Wheelock Incorporated
Builder: Beltway Builders (defunct)
Photographers:
Cesar Lujan: Pages 17, 18, 19, 20, 21, 23, 26, 27, 29
Harlan Hambright: Pages 24, 25

Sagamore Farm
Project Manager: Daniel Blair
Landscape Architect: McKee Carson Landscape Architects
Builder: Precise Buildings LLC
Photographer: Cesar Lujan

Oakhaven Farm
Builder: Advance Construction
Stonemason: George Salinas
Photographers:
Tre Dunham: Pages 41, 45, 48
Cesar Lujan: Pages 43, 47
Monica Adams: Page 49

Ketchen Place Farm
Project Manager: Cesar Lujan
Builder: Advance Construction
Photographer: Cesar Lujan

Devine Ranch
Project Manager: Mike Ezban
Builder: Crocker Homes Inc.
Photographer: Paul Schraub

Lucky Jack Farm
Project Manager: Daniel Blair
Local Architect: Allard Jensen Architects, Inc.
Interior Design: GeGe Pender Interior Design
Landscape Architect: Theresa Clark Landscape Architect
Builder: G.W. Scott Construction Inc.
Photographers:
David Hartig: Pages 73, 74, 75, 79 right, 80, 82–83, 83 right, 85
Paul Body: Pages 76–77, 78–79

River Farm

    Project Manager: Adam McGraw

    Builder: Advance Construction

    Photographers:

        Maxwell MacKenzie: Pages 87, 88 bottom, 89, 90, 91, 93, 94 bottom, 96 bottom

        Kenneth M. Wyner: Page 97

        Cesar Lujan: Pages 88 top, 94 top

Beechwood Stables

    Project Manager: Ian Kelly

    Local Architect: Marcus Gleysteen Architects

    Interior Design: SLC Interiors

    Landscape Architect: Gregory Lombardi Design

    Builder: Kenneth Vona Construction Inc.

    Photographer: Kenneth M. Wyner

Pegaso Farm

    Project Manager: Cesar Lujan

    Builder: Advance Construction

    Photographer: Cesar Lujan

All's Well Farm

    Project Manager: Amadeo Bennetta

    Interior Design: Cebula Design

    Landscape Architect: Keith LeBlanc Landscape Architecture

    Builder: Advance Construction

    Photographers:

        Cesar Lujan: Pages 127, 128, 129, 130, 131, 134, 135

        Eric Stromquist: Page 133

Private Ranch, Montana

    Project Manager: Mike Ezban

    Builder: Martel Construction

    Photographer: Cesar Lujan

Great Road Farm

    Project Manager: Ian Kelly

    Landscape Architect: Graham Landscape Architecture

    Builder: Lewis Barber Construction LLC and Kistler Buildings

    Photographer: Cesar Lujan

Glenwood Farm

    Project Manager: Cesar Lujan

    Builder: Advance Construction

    Photographer: Cesar Lujan

Private Stable, California

    Project Manager: Daniel Blair

    Local Architect: Three Square Design Studios, LLP

    Landscape Architect: Joni L. Janecki & Associates, Inc.

    Photographer: Cesar Lujan

Closing Pages

    Photographers:

        Cesar Lujan: Page 178

        Kenneth M. Wyer: Page 179